C903021815

KT-147-353

barefoot pilgrimage

ANDREA CORR

barefoot pilgrimage

A MEMOIR

HarperCollins*Publishers*

HarperCollins*Publishers*
1 London Bridge Street
London SE1 9GF

www.harpercollins.co.uk

First published by HarperCollins*Publishers* 2019

1 3 5 7 9 10 8 6 4 2

Text © Andrea Corr 2019

Photographs courtesy of the author with the following exceptions:
p.104 © Darren Kidd/Shutterstock; p.124 © Hayley Madden/Shutterstock;
p.161 Ofer Wolfberger/Getty Images; p.168 Everett Collection Inc/Alamy
Stock Photo; p.173 Amy Graves/Wire Image/Getty Images; p.174 © Alastair
Muir/Shutterstock; p.178 Andrea Corr and Peter Gaynor in the Gate
Theatre Production of Charlotte Brontë's *Jane Eyre*; p.202 © Mark Doyle;
p.208 © John Reynolds.

Andrea Corr asserts the moral right to be
identified as the author of this work

A catalogue record of this book is
available from the British Library

ISBN 978-0-00-832130-7

Printed and bound in Great Britain by
CPI Group (UK) Ltd, Croydon

MIX
Paper from
responsible sources
FSC **FSC™ C007454**
www.fsc.org

For Brett and especially for our two great blessings, Brett Jr and Jeanie. This baton passes to you.

Dear reader,

I did not sit down to write a book. This (whatever this may be) began in the summer of 2017. Two years after Daddy had died. Eighteen years after Mum. An overwhelming need to write it all down because if I died now too, this strange, normal, family, human love story as it really was to me, might also die. And then would it have ever really been?

I did not sit down at all, nor consider a destination. I just obeyed the pictures as they came. The questions. The fleeting moments. The present into the past. The present because of the past and back again with a few human, mad-gene detours along the way.

The first story – in the chalet in Skerries – was truly the first door that opened. That dusty room on top of the mattresses, hiding and pretending I wasn't there. It persisted and it seems to me now insisted I write it down. Not another one. Not a perhaps 'better' one. That memory was the first door. The first room. And it began this barefoot pilgrimage.

I walked fast to summon the pictures. I walked fast to slow them down. To still them ultimately and to merely describe, then, the room that I had returned to in my mind. A sympathetic, non-judgemental voyeur of my own life as I lived it growing up. A narrator with the blessing of hindsight. It is what it is and that is OK.

So many of the rooms I loved. They made me laugh out loud, remembering us as we were. That's a lucky thing to say. Other rooms of course I was happy to write myself out of as swiftly as possible and scramble in the dark for another door.

I tried not to think of you, dear reader, for I am a singer with a debilitating desire to be liked. I tried not to censor it all, clean and smiling like a pop video.

It came to obsess me in a way, once I began. Images from the past were appearing all the time.

Blinding flashes of you startle me awake.

The outside tap on the wall. The musty earth smell of my cat's paws. The hanging lamp over the oval glass table that you pull down and change the mood of the kitchen ... But most of all, Mum.

In my first draft she was barely there. I thought I had forgotten her. That I had forgotten what it was like to be with her. To blissfully take her for granted. But she came back to me on these walks and I think after all that it may have been she that had me do this. Because this does not feel like it was ever a decision of mine and now that I am sitting down writing to you, I think I may understand this first story. I felt a pain in my heart when I heard her voice looking for me. All this time maybe it is me that has been looking for her. And this is Jean Bell's engraving in the tree.

Take a picture with words.

Click.

My tanned feet, their nails the colour of the pool before me, the sky above. My naked three-year-old (naked babies I dreamed of) singing while he makes muddy puddles (oh, Peppa Pig and her silly dada, the 'expert') with this rented garden's hose, on this holiday in Portugal.

I'm on my third book and in my head I'm beginning my own story. Maybe I should. Maybe I can do more than the mere minutes of a song, and I can leave it to you to imagine the melody. Catchy pop with more hooks than a what was it …? But I warn you. My weakness is vanity. I want you to like me. So I must picture this unread.

Not all that I remember I am proud of, but when it comes to childhood, I think we can only wonder why, but never blame, and I think there's a continuous thread that just might explain me, but I still don't understand. And good God could we just stop analysing ourselves. First-world vocation. And Ireland says, 'Aye, that's Catholic guilt.'

The thread. I'm seven, on top of a pile of old mattresses. I can't even kneel here without touching the ceiling and I'm reading a children's book I loved, *The Wild Swans*. It's a chalet in Skerries, all blue and pink like a playhouse, cardboard walls and perpetual Fisher Price family sound. It's dusty up here, all close and hidden. I hear Mum in the kitchen and what I'm trying to get at here, Caroline's voice asking Mum has she seen me. She's calling my name down the wooden-toy hall but I keep quiet and still and she doesn't know about here, I don't think, so I stay hidden. And silent as the breath I won't exhale. This makes me sad but it's just what it is and it's just a story; she runs out calling my name, the cardboard door swinging shut, looking for me.

And this unwinds with life and lots in between to my twenty-six-year-old self, for the first time, watching a camcorder video of our lost mum, Jean, on a boat in California ... her voice at my ear so immediate it's like it rocks me awake:

'Where's Pandy?'

And my heart is wrung.

To hear a voice from the dead looking for you. To miss a voice. To miss being looked for. This means something but I don't know what.

If this is the beginning of the book I warn you, I have to leave lots out and then maybe you can say, 'Ah, but I want to read the book she didn't write.' Or maybe not. Maybe 'I

6

don't even want to read that one, thanks very much.' Now that is the inner chorus of a Dundalk girl who's come down with a dose of the 'Who do you think you are?'s.

I have to write this now though. I am scared of people dying. Actually, not people: I am scared of Johnny dying, and he has to read, counsel, manage and sell if he loves it, or not at all. Oh there's that dishcloth heart again, wrung out and reaching the base of my throat where sobs and yells gather to consider their escape.

Not now.

I'd like to say I always wrote but I'd be lying. There were girls like that in my class, writing poetry because they couldn't help it and getting published, albeit in our school magazine. I got my first A in honours English in my Leaving Cert. Believe me, it wasn't coming and it was a shock, but I did know I wrote my best story, that hot June day in the exam hall (why was it always hot for exams and not for holidays?). I actually laughed out loud writing it (*shhhh … sorry*) and enjoyed it more than anything before. And the world went quiet, as it does now.

'Soap Opera: Suds or something more significant?' The latter of course.

And I'd like to thank that boiled egg Mammy made me and the bottle of Lucozade I had with my friend Conor before I went in.

* * *

These are bewildering times I find my forty-three-year-old self in. And I can give you my views, though they're just the conversation you had last night. We're about to release our T Bone Burnett record, *Jupiter Calling*. I did think we should consider calling it *Love in a Time of Terror*, but let's let music and words do what they will to you personally. Bring you where you uniquely want and here is a place you may not wish to be reminded of …

That other title, though, is the truth of what this record means. Where hate is incited from the most powerful pulpits, we cry 'Bulletproof Love'. You hear, 'Go home, you're not getting in'; we drown it out with 'SOS'.

Love in a time of profound disappointment and degradation. I think of words, meaning and evolution. Humankind. I'm only human. When did 'kind' slip out and 'only' skulk in? We've swapped aspiration for resignation. Our humanity now, a mere excuse.

And our small failings posed, posted and applauded. A million likes in one hour for a cosmetically altered sixteen-year-old pout (surely that's not right, Doctor? Mother?). I don't blame the girl (childhood, remember?) but what will we become?

Darwin, wait – we're going the wrong way!

But also I might die and Daddy wrote his memoir and his daddy before him. He, James Corr, lived through two world wars. ('Why am I reading *this*? Where can I get his?' *Voce piena*, chorus to fade …)

8

You see, my life is permanently passing before my very eyes these days. It's all near death.

The inhalations! The cold and present breath and the memory in my lungs. Earthly light. Moment. Isness. Human love. Meaning. Here. The body. The swirl and the electricity of the heart, beating away by itself on the eco cycle in a night light while you sleep … even … Sleep. So worthy of a mention here, though so often looked down upon …

Sleep is beautiful …

That's the thing when you wake up a forty-year-old orphan … fear of that loss, of time running out, of ending, knowingly repeating the same stories, 'memory lane' as Daddy called them, just to have them in the room again … and I suppose that means I love life, I love human beings, I love strangers so much sometimes I get a pain in my heart … You lovely lady on the crutch that I came to from my thoughts to realise I hadn't held the door open for … I went back; 'Sorry!' I said, and held it, only for the buggy with my boy in it to topple over.

'No good deed goes unpunished,' you smiled into my eyes.

And therein may lie the poetry of human existence, I think. The reach of another someone, someone you didn't see before and may never see again. However, it's not all beautiful. I just passed a man bulling his way down the Fulham Road, banging into a woman, all Him and His

9

Rucksack ... and their head-nodding verbal exchange thereafter ...

Anyway, that said, I still love you, stranger. Fellow human, sharing this faulty planet at the same time.

Mum, a Donegal girl, and Dad, Dundalk born and bred, met at a dance hall in Blackrock: The Pavilion, it was called. She was twenty-one and he thirty … He fixed an eeny-meeny-miny-moe to land on her to dance, and wrote a poem about the destiny and the 'what if's involved.

Booze bored
Winter woed
Bed beckoning
Did angels convene
To bring me to Jean
Of wraparound eyes
In passion of pink
First dance
Last dance
We dance forever ...

And they did. I'm not saying it was uninterrupted bliss, kiss and laughter … oh they could fight too, but isn't the fight, in reality, just a different step?

They talked of a pivotal moment. They were at the pictures on a date, when 'Strangers on the Shore' played and there it was: recognition, a mutual love of music.

And their shared life rolled out before them.

The other day I found a letter he wrote her, folded up in a box in his bedroom in Dundalk. He is funny throughout, as always he was, and quotes her – 'you're very bold, Gerry', admonishing his wicked sense of humour but also loving it and sharing it, all at the same time. But in the last paragraph he writes:

I find it difficult, Jean, to communicate on paper my feelings for you. True love like great music is beyond the reach of words. Suffice it to say then, that I wish to spend the rest of my life being good to you, to you my love, today tomorrow and always. Ps write soon please?

They had five children. Our brother Gerard, born next after Jim, was killed on the road in front of our house, in the very first days after they had brought the new baby, Sharon, home from hospital. While Mum showed her off to our aunt Maureen, he avoided the locked gates by hopping over our neighbour's wall and ran out after a ball. The car stopped, but it hit him while moving off once again, presuming he would wait and wouldn't run back. He was three years old.

Now that I have two children of my own, I find I have no eloquence here … it is too unbearable. So this will be short.

Throughout their lives our parents could not exceed three minutes talking of him. The pain would arrest them all too soon. Therefore I don't have many stories, but what I do know I will tell you.

Gerard was funny, the image of Dad, and, it would seem to me, clever beyond his years. On being told, one day, that his shoes were on the wrong feet, he crossed his legs and smiled up at them … 'They're on the right feet now,' he said. He would sit on his chair in the kitchen and ask for more toast, more tea (he liked tea) and, feeling Daddy's impatience, he would repeat, 'More tea, more toast,' in a convincing sing-song voice, only to respond to Daddy's disbelieving 'Och' with an 'Only joking!'

He was also a great singer and now it has me thinking of the destiny and the what ifs ... Would he have been the lead singer of a band ... A family trio ... Jim, Gerard and Sharon ...

Caroline and myself, a dream they never had.

'April 3 1970'

Set me free
Why would I want to hurt you
When I love you
When your blood is mine?
Why would I want to be the thorn in your side
Hold you back from your life
Be the shadow in your light?
I am in the state of bliss
And I am love
That's all I am in you
I am your purest love
Set me free

Would you want that for me
Would you haunt a child on his journey to man
Would you blame a little boy
Would you wish you were alive?
Set me free brother
My love is your light
It's in your fingers on the keys
In your song, your melody
I am you and you are me
And we will see eternity
Set me free
And you'll be free
April 3 1970

There is much that winks and sparkles in a Monet light. And I am Thumbelina tripping across the lily pads … The Children of Lir, the Salmon of Knowledge. The washing blowing on the line, hiding my face in the honeyed pink light of the sheets. Or am I lying on the sheets, cradled in summer smells. Looking up at my mum and the floating white in the blue.

Pocket money for the carefully chosen penny sweets and the 'Och' that escapes the wicked shopkeeper as the bell tolls our arrival after Sunday Mass. For time is money and time is just 30p today.

Swingball, the paddling pool, breathe in Daddy's face, all petrol and grass after he's mown the lawn in straight lines. Hopscotch hop over the fence to my next-door neighbour and early-childhood best friend Paul, don't let the wire catch, fish-hooked in your bottom lip like poor twister Caroline did and knock knock knock … Spilled milk and a drowning fly for the cats by the door … The sound of Violet's radio – 'wireless' – within, she aproned and singing along, keeping her country with Big Tom … Paul's heavy flip-flop-flap-slap running free down the hall while a dishwater Mammy hand proffers a sunken queen cake, 'Ye wee pet'. Make a mental note to disappear before the same loving hand spoons out the cod liver oil. And out the door we run to play to …

'Paul, your coooaaaaaaaaaaaat …'

… the cement mixer and the delicious slop for our cookery kitchen.

'Here's one I made earlier' – Paul's best Delia voice as our culinary mud and dandelion creation appears behind the tile door of the brick fridge. Oh, the joys of having a best friend as your next-door neighbour and a dad that is not Bob, but is Tom the builder. The see-saw, a seven-foot, smooth, splinter-free beam of wood on a barrel with more solid grey bricks for breaks, lets you bump your bum happy and he's lifting off sky high into seventh heaven … Walk-run, (but not too fast coz it will go all cartoon Road Runner on you), scuff-toed, Clarks sturdy shoes on those barrels now for the barrel race and circus time. Kick the can, hide-and-seek, blind man's buff, climb the trees, night fern smells on my blackened palms and at home later I am still a part of my friend's life. I hear the slate shovel dragging and slurping in the coal and slack for the fire now, because their house is always kept warm, even in the summer. Always a fire lit. Sure she sunbathes her white talcum puff skin beneath a hat and a wool plaid blanket. While our black Irish, Spanish-invasion mammy next door is brown as a berry and sleek, smelling of Ambre Solaire.

17

And the doors are closing, night night ... Stories, memories and pictures merge and spring vivid, only to dissipate ... But there is a shadow. I see it. Yes, of course.

Because I realise now that all that time there was a ghost in our house. And there was one next door, too. Another missing boy named Brian who gets caught in Violet's throat telling Paul to put on his coat and pull up his hood. 'Ah Paul, you'll catch your death,' as if death really was catching ... Don't allow your first glance at the full moon to accidentally fall through your pane of glass. We are on our knobbly knees holding on to the bursting dam of a laugh through the Angelus and the rosary at six o'clock. A revolving, weary-go-round string of prayers and endless blessing of oneself, in the name of the Father and of the Son and of the Holy Spirit, hand wings flutter swift over heart, Father Son Holy Spirit, bowing heads and pray for us, Father Son Holy Spirit, beads to lips, three holy trinity kisses, bless lips, bless forehead, bless heart, again, again, again as if asking, pleading, 'How many times will keep us safe and here, tell me, Father Son Holy Spirit, so I can seal us all in for the evening, sacred and sound, Amen.'

Our very own beautiful and beloved ghost, our own missing one behind Mammy's brown eyes benign. A little boy standing next to Jim. Two little boys had two little toys. In her squeezing-tighter hand crossing the road. In her pause before the tunnel bridge, yielding right of way to the train about to thunder overhead.

Out of your mind with grief: it's a good line. I hear that many relationships do not survive the death of their child. I'd say survive remains the one right word in this brutal sentence for at least a very long time. Condemned to life … missing … It makes sense really. Maybe you could pretend you're still the happy, naive and untouched by the darkness twenty-eight-year-old you were a matter of days before, if you don't look the loss in the eyes any more. But no … You couldn't even … The wrench in your chest and the yearning … No, I won't go there now. I'll close that door. But they had no choice. Door always blowing open; a wailing, crying mouth and a cot in the echoing emptiness within. *A foot for every year* …

Gerard Corr
12 August 1966 – 3 April 1970

'Jean and Gerard' by Gerry Corr

Last night you cried
Remembering him
Your tears pierced the ice
Of numbed remembrance
And I fled
Like always

I wish I could stay
And essay his perfection
On the faltering steps of love
Like before

Tear-racked morning eyes
Watch new buds leap
From dead clematis
As new essays
In lost perfection
Assuage the pain
Once again

I inhale September deeper than any other month. I hold its breath and repeat, 'I love this time of year' as surely as I'll say 'Merry Christmas' in December. The happiest sound is a playground swarm on the bell. The fallen leaves and the conkers. And with the outside foggy cold on my own children's cheeks, I breathe into my first days at school.

The Redeemer School was a five-minute walk from our house. Árd Easmuinn, the area in which we lived, shared a primary school with what was a council estate called Cox's Demesne. It was a sprawling rectangular bungalow of classrooms off corridors and right angles on corners. Every turn an afterthought. I see blue walls, maps of Ireland, stripy straws spilled on the linoleum floor, coloured crucifix links, sycamore leaf rubbings and my Moses project. I smell márla – our play-dough – the thick red and yellow gloop of paint, newsprint, fat crayons and a cloakroom at the back of the class.

'An bhfuil cead agam dul go dti an leitreas, más é do thoil é?'

22

The, till now, unsolved mystery of the puddle beneath the chair.

'*Ní raibh cead agam ...*'

And something sacred to me then, that I cannot grasp now: a rectangular box. What did it house? It swam to the top when I watched *Krapp's Last Tape*. Something intangible but fantastic to me.

There are triangular cartons of milk on a shelf and lessons that don't include spellings or times tables. Firstly I realised that I was a short-haired girl here and not a boy. It dawned on me at around the same time as I discovered that my desk mate, Julie, with corduroy trousers beneath a skirt, was a girl.

I met my best friend Niamh on my first day and our lives have walked down parallel hawthorn-hedged lanes ever since. Our unrequited and disappointing loves engraved on the seen-it-all-before, though bent in sympathy, secret-keeping trees. Our hands reach out every now and then, and back we go to the field after the drinks cabinet and the Dolly Mixtures, the stone wall and a song about a green puppet called ...

Orville?

Yes?

Who is your very best friend?

You are!

I'm gonna help you mend ...

Rice Krispies in the bowl but didn't you eat cornflakes ...?

We both call each other Bosom, as in bosom buddies from *Anne of Green Gables*, and we still do. We grew differently however ... Well, let's just say that she alone grew into our name.

All grown up, we lose each other one day around Grafton Street in Dublin and then simultaneously find each other. She is outside Davy Byrnes. I'm outside The Bailey.

'BOSOM!!' we shout and the doorman beside me gives us both a good look over as she crosses to my side.

He says to me with his mobile eyes unblinking, 'I can understand why she's called Bosom, but why the hell are you called Bosom?!'

Ah, she's had her ups and downs, my Bosom. A newspaper got a detail wrong once (it happens sometimes) and gave the ecstatic news that my best friend 'Busty' was to be my fourth bridesmaid.

Up the Town

'Well!' is how we said hello in Dundalk: an exclamation rather than a question.

An oddly hopeful 'How are ye?' when the auto-response was more often than not: 'Strugglin'.'

Or Dad's and my favourite: 'Ah, same ole shit, another day.'

We would later abbreviate this to 'SOS'.

'How are you, Daddy?'

'Ah, SOS, Pandy. How are you?'

And one day, my hand in his, walking up the town, he said to a man going by, 'How's the form?'

And I looked up and asked, 'Has that man got a farm, Daddy?'

We would walk on the dark, cold early evenings, frost steaming from our talk, and do a crawl of the churches to see the baby Jesus in the manger. New born in the hay, in a red glow of light.

And there was the weekly scram to twelve o'clock Mass, for Daddy's above at the organ, you see, looking through the mirror for our heads bent in prayer. His dark wee angels. If he didn't spot your head you could allay his suspicion later, with the mention of a bum note peeking cheeky out of Bach. Well, it was bound to be true.

Mammy eventually stopped attending Mass. She said sitting there made her panic.

But now I look back and realise that a lot of people were, in truth, struggling at this time in Dundalk. This was the late 70s, early 80s. The milk at the back of the classroom was necessary. There were a lot of single-parent households with dads away, peacekeeping in the Lebanon. Of course I was a child. I had no real notion, then, of any household being different to our own. One mum at home plus one dad at work until he returned to do the peace-keeping you just couldn't mute the way you could hers. And to give you a piano lesson.

But it must have been very hard. Years later, I met a girl I'd known at that school who told me of a time when they literally ran out of food and that milk was all they had. I remember a friend of Sharon's who put me on a stool beside him by our cooker and turned making 'the thickest ever pancakes!' into a game.

Pride, it seems, can be the last casualty of poverty. It hurts my heart to think of it now. I didn't know he was hungry.

Dundalk became a refuge for Catholics who had been burned out of their homes in 1969. The burning of Bombay Street. One of the council estates, Muirhevnamor, became known locally as Little Belfast and it was understood that there were places you did not go, unless you 'sympathised'.

And then of course the border, the soldiers, and Daddy's wicked sense of humour. Jim in the back of the car as it slowed … Mum complaining to Dad, 'Oh Gerry, I hate seeing these men with guns.'

And Daddy responding, 'Don't worry, Jean. They only want little boys.'

Poor Jim. That was too bold, Gerry.

Although I can still see the H-block graffiti glaring and desperate on the grey, ominous brick of the tunnel bridge, beneath the train track, generally I was as oblivious to the ongoing conflict as I was to the hunger. Not surprising, really … I was a full and happy child.

But no matter what, you still grow in the soil you've been planted in and here, I discovered that morality, right and wrong, can be complicated and confusing.

The Baddies and the Goodies

For some reason, Caroline and myself would often be early for school and we would play with the caretaker, who we loved. Then one day he wasn't there any more and the Redeemer School was on the news. They had discovered weapons hidden in the roof of the assembly room.

'But that was a goodie doing the work of a baddie?'

I happened to be born in Dundalk on the day of the deadliest attack of the Troubles in the Republic.

On 17 May 1974, four car bombs exploded at rush hour in Dublin and Monaghan, killing thirty-three people and a full-term unborn child. I have discovered since that my father-in-law, Dermot, just missed being in Talbot Street the moment the bomb exploded. He was to buy a bottle of shampoo for his young wife, Pat, in a pharmacy on North Earl Street, just a hundred yards from where the bomb would go off. But it being a beautiful day, he decided to keep on walking and buy it closer to home. As he turned off Talbot Street on to Amiens Street his ears rang deaf and the ground shook beneath his feet.

Bold Gerry, Baa and the Outstretched Contrite Hand

Once upon a time there lived a husband and a father who had a wicked sense of humour. He was possessed of many gifts, not least of all being sporty as a youth. However, one day, his curious, rebellious soul led his fit but mortal coil into his dying sister's forbidden Victorian sick room. She, Eileen, a dark-haired white form, lay on the bed with a bleeding cough and a fire in each cheek. Some time later, Eileen having departed, Gerry (for that was the name of the young man) found himself chronically tired and not at all able for his Gaelic football or his tennis. When his new friend Dolphin Cough, Eileen's old bestie, started pulling red flags from his mouth, he was quickly dispatched to the sanitarium for eleven months wherein he made his living, not dying, as a bookie and had a romance with a nurse. And luckily for all of us (or was it?) was just in time for Waksman's cure: streptomycin.

In the meantime, a shy girl was begotten and born to William and Lizzy. When she turned fifteen William would depart, his time-bomb heart tick-tocking him into the Great Unknown. And Lizzy would out-linger, though her brain would depart on the early train to beyond, long before her body would follow. She, clad in shoes, a skirt and a blouse beneath a cross-your-heart, Father Son Holy Spirit, bra.

Jean (for that was the young maiden's name) was beautifully unaware of her growing beauty, gap-toothed and lost as she was in the cloud of testosterone she and her three sisters predominantly inhaled.

6 hungry boys + 4 potatoes each makes 7 million peelings old ...

'What happened to your hands, Nanna?'

'I put them in the fire, Caroline.'

'Did you put your face in the fire, too?'

... and only the girls paying keep ... Well I think I'll just go and boil a head of lettuce and get it over with. Inhalations were deeper on McSwiney Street than elsewhere, and exhalations late.

You see, when God looked up from Jean's incisors, he got transfixed by her eyes and He threw in an infinity of love. Teeth could only mull over this wonder while enjoying a cocktail stick. But they, hard as they were, could never know this love.

Love me just a little bit and I'll cast such love on you, but I won't smile in photos. That's something I won't do.

She wore a pink dress with the velvet dusk of the Irish rose and led love into a ballroom wherein she was tricked into a dance with a charming rebel. Her jilted girlfriend left, thinking she may have in fact won, and her mouth saying, on receipt of the news from her up-down eyes:

'He has a very good-looking face but he is a bit short in the leg.'

But Jean thought that the way this beautiful man-face was looking at her more than made up for the deficit in the leg. And so they courted, he picking her up in his racing green Fiat 500 and stopping not far from McSwiney Street where they kissed and she told him that she loved his face.

'So do ye think ye might marry me someday?' he said, and she laughed at the irony of the man with all the words, having so few.

'Shelling Hill' by Gerry Corr

You'd be blessed to find it; down tortuous track
Hardly the breadth of Cooley's fabled hero,
Not to mention Maeve's brown bull.
From the beginning it was our private place
Our little car, almost without bidding,
Bringing us there each Sunday

One day a cow came by,
Drawn not by the scent of forbidden fruit
But by blameless apple,
Mooing an end to our caresses
Passion and laughter not a good mix.
Poor bedfellows, you might say.

We laughed again on another day
When words unbidden dropped in on us
'Do you think you might marry me one day?'
I swear a passing dog smiled,
The ocean roared, of course,
And the Lord of sky beamed a blessing.
My lady trembled a little
As in girlish excitement
Until a giggle breached it's frantic confine
And we took refuge in each other's arms.
'Who said that?' I said, and we laughed
And laughed, and laughed.

Cupid's cheeky chariot joined in later
Rocking and rolling us
Home to Dundalk ...

22 February 2000

And all would be content ever after but for Gerry having a penchant for revealing the gap teeth.

He thought that if God, when pouring in lashings of love, had not mixed in equal measures of hope and fear, then it might not have been so delicious to go to such wicked measures. But then again, if easily won, would it have been so rewarding?

Years passed as they do in Grimm fairytales. Jean's tummy grew and grew, again and again and again, and out came Jim Gerard Sharon Caroline and Andrea. A family band.

'This is PG' Grimm thought for the very first time, and hoped they'd forget the second boy Gerard. And so ...

Hope, Fear and the Beetroot

One day a guttural and terrifying scream did interrupt the fledglings at their various offices above and had them racing down the stairs to see ...

... their father doubled over by the open door of the fridge, coughing into a pool of blood! With mouths open and poised to join their petrified mother in this primitive and tribal chorus, they observed that the cough had morphed into a laugh ... For one could not miss opportunities when they presented themselves so beautifully, he thought ... We don't cry over spilled milk ... but poor Mammy does ... All over the spilled juice from a jar of pickled beetroot.

Baa.

Sorry, Jean.

The Cross Pen

It must be acknowledged that the father, though terribly cuddly, was betimes a grumpy daddy.

'You're in a bad mood again, Daddy.'

'I AM NOT IN A BAD MOOD!!!'

Various sounds and head-jerks alerted us to his internal weather system. Grumbles and groans, muted thunder and bolts, and the head jolting twice, three times to the left with the assumed objective of loosening an invisible suffocating collar and tie. Or a noose, perhaps.

He appeared home from work this day with the aspect of a man whose inner sky has clouded over an oppressive grey.

'Have any of you seen my Cross pen?'

One can only imagine now the afflicted individual who, on opening his bag at work earlier, discovered to his chagrin the aforesaid missing biro. And therein the brew began ...

'No, Daddy.'

And so it was daily for approximately eight bewildered days, with the question gathering variants in meaning and expression, such as:

'Did any of you *take* my Cross pen?'

And punctuated with 'Ach's' galore.

'Ach!'

On perhaps the sixth day I had found myself deeply fatigued with the Cross pen, so I decided to say:

'No, I haven't seen your Cross pen,' just when he had begun the refrain, 'Did any o—'

'No.'

On the eighth day we duetted again, according to the scripture, except this was different.

'Lo, what's this?' I remarked to myself. 'My longest exhausted noooooooooooooo has failed to put an end to today's song?'

'Everyone, I want you to check your school bags for my Cross pen.'

'Tssk, Daddy, it's not in my school bag! I didn't take your stupid [inner voice … as that, I am not] Cross pen!'

'Just check it, Andrea.' (Weather warning: Pandy when cuddly, Andrea when not.)

So poor wee me drags my school bag in with my own weather. My ochs and huffs and blows and I start to pull stuff out of my bag. I really am above all this carry-on now, when … wait … what is that shine of silver peeping out of Bran, my riveting reading book?

Oh …

I just could not understand it. I ran off crying.

'I still feel bad about that one, Pandy. That one took a while.'

Baa.

Inherited Wickedness

And so we did it too, to each other, and admittedly I fear I was the worst because:

'You're boring me now, Andrea,' was as regular as the Angelus.

Oh, the Angelus always makes me think funny thoughts. You know the visual montage they play on the TV to the sound of the dong-dongs? Random people in various jobs putting down tools, if they have any, and pausing to reflect on God (as ye do at six o'clock every day)?

The farmer turning off the tractor, looking up to the right at … I presume God, but we don't actually see Him (oh that's something to reflect on right there … it's working!).

The mammy (there she is again) resting on her hoover to look out the window at the tweety birds circling … (or are they above her head, haha).

Nature, nature, glorious nature. It's everywhere!

Babbling brooks, migrating swallows, potatoes being picked with earthy, black, return-of-the-native nails.

And when Ireland recognised that God loves all his children and got the chance to see many of them in real life (long live the one hundred thousand welcomes, and when faced with this chance to give thanks, may we never forget the *céad mile fáiltes* a million of our own starving refugees needed), as Ireland grew and changed, so too did the montage …

Now we have a Chinese lady looking up from her office desk (killed two isms with the one stone there) and I'm not even on the funny thoughts yet but you have them too, don't you?

The man pausing his unrolling of the toilet roll to look up and ponder ...

What are you supposed to do if the Angelus strikes then, tell me?

Eh, hold on a second now, God.

(He made me like this ... God, I mean.

Hi, have I been introduced yet? No – ye left me out, of course ye did.

I'm Guilt.)

... Toes mid-curl at bottom of dishevelled, silken and moving, two-headed monster.

Baa.

Sorry, God.

Ahhhh! Air traffic control!!

Hmm. For some, the pause for the Angelus should most definitely not be observed.

'Ellis Island'

On the second Sunday
Annie be my guide
Liberty's a welcome
To an aching eye
We'll grow up together
Far away from home

38

Crossed the sea and ocean
To the land of hope
Kingstown to Liverpool
Crossing the Irish Sea
You gotta keep your wits on you
Where you lay your head
Six minute medical
Leaving no chalk on me
Goodbye Ellis Island
Hello land of free

Every man and woman
Every boy and girl
Sing out Ellis Island
Sing a song of hope
Sing for us together
Sing we're not alone
Sing we'll go back someday
Sing we will belong

When the leaves are falling
And the sky is on the ground
We will come together
And sing of Ireland
Thanking Ellis Island
Thank you USA
You gave us a home here
Crying a brand new day

Queenstown to New York Bay
Wild Atlantic Ocean
You gotta keep your wits on you
Where you lay your head
Six minute medical
Leaving no chalk on me
Goodbye Ellis Island
Hello land of free ...

Did they really do it to me, though?

If I'm honest, my only memorable humiliation was thinking we were all still playing hide-and-seek when they'd forgotten me, a thumb-sucking curl that Jim had manoeuvred into the top of the hot press ... Ahhh, cradled in winter smells ... Yum yum.

They didn't even pronounce me missing.

I was likely found following another 'Where's Pandy?'

Thank you, Mammy.

But I had a nose for under your skin that wasn't natural in a child.

Poor Mammy, she must have been going through the Change (distant screaming far off), because she screamed at every little thing.

'Ahhhh!!!!' was to be heard at regular intervals, and a few petrified, hair-raising:

'Gerry!!!!!!'s

'Ahhhhhhhhhh!!!!!!'

'Gerry!!!!!!' ... I'm actually doing it again ...

... I'd fall down on the ground and writhe in agony for her ...

'Gerry!!!!!!!!!!!!!!!!!!!!'

'Ahhhhhhhhhhhhhhhhhhhhhhhhhhhhhhhhhhhhhhhhhhhh-hhhhhhhhhhhhhhhhh!!!' Fighting the invisible bogeymen away from my twisting, turning, don't-touch-me! head ...

'Noooooooooooooooooooooooooooooooooo!!!!!'

What could it be? I needed to be prepared for all eventualities ...

So what if it was just that she saw Caroline's scrambled egg pot from earlier still sitting yellow and curdled in the sink ... She'd told the bitch to CLEAN IT NOW fifteen minutes ago. But to me, then, life was like a disowned rucksack in a train station ... You never know.

Baa.

Sorry, Mammy.

Comeuppance imminent, Pandy

And Jim was ... How can I put it? Addictive. Yes, that's it.

He was packing shelves in Tesco, on parole for not sitting his Leaving Cert. You see, he actually stood it up.

(I'd tripped over his school bag too many times, on my way to Paul's, to not understand what they were roaring about inside. And to understand why he was grounded. Then I worked out that the grounding must be elsewhere because we can't find Jim in his room and a window is open.)

And he had a TASCAM 244 studio in his purple bedroom with all of the manuals just waiting for him to feast on and get to know intimately.

It was a very difficult time. The artist's Tesco blue period, I could say.

I honestly can hear a violin!

Oh, forget it. That's just Sharon in her room.

How embarrassing.

Jim was 'not in a good place right now', as they say, and every day he awoke to find his nightmare was reality.

Now I love everyone here, you know that? It's just a twitch.

I'm just as God made me.

Shhhhhhhhhhhhhhhhhhhh …

There was a hand gesture (no, not what you're thinking, but).

A hand gesture, unique. (If you have interactive, press red now.)

It didn't have sound, mostly; for mostly, it didn't need it. And you wouldn't want to be relying on that, when sometimes he is already on his way, in his prison blue overall, to pack the shelves (Andrex Quilted today) and he thinks it's over and that he has won and that I couldn't possibly be at the window now … but look!

I'm there.

I start with a serene, otherworldly smile, as if one has passed but is at peace. I am sublime and I am prophetic.

And then one discerns a subtle hand gesture emerging from my sleeve. A gesture that wouldn't make sense to most and was a method of tortuous teasing unique to us. Like the ghost of the bird that is cupped in one's hand, being ever so gently rocked to sleep. And then my face, all sad, ever so sad, like it's a raindropped window through to the deep compassion and pity for my poor brother that was filling my very being ...

Baa.

Sorry, Jim.

Oh, I think I have to stop now ... This is turning into confession.

Oh no ... Don't think about it ... no.

Bless me, reader, for I have ...

I am back in Dundalk, that choppy-haired, blood-lipped, slip, red bra and Doc Marten boots time, and (though you didn't know it ... or is that what I did to make you love me?) ... I was troubled. The pain of a pop star ... you're breaking my heart.

Bosom, when she refers to it, says things like:

'Do you remember the time you drank tea, Bosom?'

Mammy must have been really worried because she came into the front room, stole my teapot, replaced it with a bottle of wine and practically locked us in.

Anyway, it's like my ears are on inside out and I'm so sick of myself that I rarely see, but the times that I do see, I take for a sign. For instance ...

I raise my coal worn eyes from my feet and realise they have opened on the Friary Church and I think I must go in … I am supposed to go in. And then lo and behold, I just happen to sit in the pew queue for confession … So …

I'm in.

The dragging wood and my heartbeat reveals the spectre behind the grid. Bowed, white-furred head, not looking, but I'm looking and I feel just awful about having to say – to lie! – 'It's been three years, Father.'

And before he could get the most gentle 'Why, my child?' out of his still-quivering-in-the-wake-of-so-many-prayers lips, I blamed him for the whole lot of it. (God … was I going through the Change?)

'I find it difficult, Father, as a woman [I had to verify that coz even if he was looking, it would still be hard to tell] to hold my head up high in this church.'

'Oh no,' he said.

Yes I do. My grandmother Alice was preached at to bear all the children God thought fit to bless her with … She had number ten at the ripe young age of forty-seven and if there was a break of more than a year between children, which apparently in Alice's story there was not, a mortified woman could be asked why she was not bringing more baby Catholics into the world and was everything all right at home, so to speak.

But back to Alice (who would later take to her bed for two years, and who needed electric shock treatment to jolt the bloodless depression out of her, once and for all)

… Not once did Daddy see her sit at the table with them and eat the food she had made. She waited. A benevolent and loving servant. A womb with no view.

I wish I could read your memoirs, Alice … I want to hear of some blessed sunshine days … There must have been some? Episodes of light beyond the low-hanging dusty grey of the honeymoon you spent cleaning Corr's Grocery before it opened in Dundalk. And the extraordinary sign-off in the postcard from James Corr, your then betrothed:

Lough Derg, 1926

Dear Alice
Having a grand time here. Came yesterday and going
    back tomorrow. Big crowd on the Island.
Goodbye
James

Ah, maybe I'm not being fair though, James. Maybe it's because everyone can read a postcard.

Daddy did make his mammy laugh, though. I know that. Because her love would shine out of her kind, blue Irish eyes. I remember that.

Father …!

Are you still listening to me?

When God smiled on one such as Alice, and blessed her with a new baby Catholic, she was not permitted to

receive the Eucharist (take Holy Communion) before she was 'churched', a baptism of sorts, to cleanse her of 'the sin of concupiscence'.

Oh no …

Do you mean that that did not happen, Father?

Oh nooooo …

And something stopped me and I felt … I feel so bad for raining on the old man's parade. He'd likely given sixty of his eighty years to his church.

I am sorry for that.

And now that I'm on this, I'm sorry for the Irish men of that time, too. Having to confess their 'impure thoughts'.

The origin of thought is pure, surely? Pure as love. Until it is corrupted and manipulated by guilt and oppression.

And we see how religion can give God a bad name.

Inherited Wickedness continued ...

I think I'll begin this one with:

Sorry, Caroline.

Baa.

Poor Caroline, Caddles the Waddles, was just too close for her own comfort (never mine). We two being quasi-Siamese, if you plee-ease ...

We shared a double bed. We wore the same clothes. A different colour (she blue and me red) sufficing to express our individualities.

We shared a name when being called:.

'Children!'

Because that in itself would bring us both, of course, having been together. And Mammy had read that book about the economising housewife (a real page-turner, apparently).

We had a secret language in which we invariably communicated through pursed-lip hums ...

MmMmMm (happily, stands for both 'Caroline' and 'Andrea')

Mm (yes)

M Mm Mm Mm m (Are you asleep? Almost a double syllable given to the 'eep' – all authentic languages having their exception to the rule.)

She cried when I was late for school. Worried face and high, uptight stance above me, still pulling my socks on, happy, at the hot press.

I, to my shame, did not react the same way to Caroline's everyday childhood troubles.

I can only excuse myself now by saying that I had no experience in worrying. She literally worried for me. She, being fourteen months older and 'the youngest mammy ever born', as they called her, took the instinct and personal need away. She did enough worrying for both of us.

This tale comprises two parts, which make up the one wicked whole. But they should demonstrate what it is I am expunging here ...

A tale of two sisters (if you like).

Part 1

At the doctor's one day, myself and my twin twister Caroline were arrested in our play to realise that we hadn't just come on this errand for the ride and must not be going shopping, which meant that we wouldn't be joining forces in breaking Mammy down into getting us a Chester cake (I have not eaten one in over thirty years, but I can taste it now ...)

Before we knew it, Caroline was up ye get, hop-upping onto the bed and taking her shoes off, wherein Dr O'Reilly examined the wee worried feet. He diagnosed:

'Fallen arches.'

'I'm worrying for two, Doctor, what do you expect?' she said.

No, that didn't happen. I think I just don't want to say this one ...

Now his diagnosis wasn't so bad in itself, obviously, but it was the remedy that got me ... The cure.

'So what do we do, Doctor?' Mammy asked.

'She will have to wear built-up shoes, Jean.'

That's all it took ... A sudden flash of an image in my brain of Caroline wearing Daddy's 70s platform shoes to school. The shoes that the itinerants, collecting, had rejected and thrown out of the black plastic sack in the baby's pram, onto the road, right in front of our house ... They couldn't even wait till they got home.

'Get them out of my sight now!'

I exploded with laughter.

'Well now, that's the bitch,' the doctor said.

Part 2

I have told you that we shared a bed. So with that in mind I will move swiftly on away from my shameful but helpless laughter in Frank O'Reilly's smoke-filled surgery to ...

(Thumbelina is sinking now)

... this.

I awoke one morning, I stretched and proceeded to look at my sleeping twister beside me. But it was not my twister ... She was in there, definitely – they were her eyes and nose, yes – but she was peeping out of the biggest human moon face you've ever imagined, sleep-crying, 'Help! Let me out!!'

'Caroline! Wake up! Your face!'

So we run to the mirror and I see her horrified eyes find themselves stuck in the moon of the mumps and I cannot help but explode. There was peeing of pants again and:

'Andrea, go to the toilet!' That 'basic human function', as Daddy described it in his wedding speech, that I could never manage to 'make time for'.

I have to admit it, because it will take them a bit to tell their side, and that was something Caroline said often. A few times a day, in fact.

But it is only right that I give something back in advance ...

A credit note float. Ha.

Oh, I feel exorcised right now.

Night night.

This morning, the door to Sharon's Baa sorry is locked like her teenage bedroom. I'm right outside and can hear the needle gently resting on 'Save a Prayer' ... not like when I do it to visions of a band scrambling to a terrified start, crashing, screeching and breaking into the song like a road accident ... And I couldn't look up to her more if she were the Eiffel Tower. She lets me in sometimes and I love it there. Perfumes and slip-on, red polka-dot shoes, and bras. And she talks to me like we are the same and not like I am just an awed spectator. Naturally hers. She sometimes puts the make-up on me from her Naturally Yours make-up case because she sells this to women in their homes these days ... Your local Avon lady.

Oh Sharon, you are my redeemer! My absolution after the remorse of confession!

I helped you!

No Baa Sha!

Running ahead of Mum, Dad and Caroline on Skerries Beach to pre-warn her of their hastening approach. So she could put out her cigarette and cram a mouthful of cinnamon Dentyne. Never ever telling when she had friends over and continued Jim's weekend 'party at the Corrs' house' tradition. When they were out playing, 'at sing'. Or when she came home one day and just couldn't stop laughing. She might have died so I helped her retire to her room, like a smuggler avoiding the customs. So they wouldn't worry, of course.

I was her alibi and her ally and she was mine.

She sent her boyfriend to MJ's, the pub I was in, to get me out of it … To come home early, at least, (and soften the 'deal with you later' landing …) from 'wherever' I was, when I was not babysitting the two kids Dad had just said hello to, contentedly eating JR ice pops with their mother.

Confidences, consolation and 'you are not alone's in her room.

No Baa Sha is my sister-friend.

And when we tickled her on the kitchen floor she was the one with the kicking 'piranha legs' …

God knows.

Gerry Was a Holy Joe

Daddy considered being a priest, apparently. Stories of their parish priest coming to visit them and of having tea in the good china in 'the good room' (the room, and indeed the china, reserved for holy priest visits and the like) with his mother, Alice, who was – remarkably to me – very religious still. (Before falling in love with James, it was thought that she would become a nun.) She and James walked to six o'clock Mass every morning in the Redemptorist Church, before they opened the shop and even the year before she died they both made their annual Lough Derg pilgrimage ... But with Daddy it was a kind of courtship, I hear. And to have a priest in the family was seen as a great blessing. It didn't, of course, come to pass, but he remained the holiest Joe in our house of God and the odd sermon he gave us, including Mammy the girl, was indeed priestlike ... He played the organ every Sunday in the Redeemer Church. *Jesu, joy of man's desiring, Awake* ... Sharon, when being reprimanded for being late for Mass one Sunday, called him 'a religious fanatic' (he was ahead of his time) and Mammy burst out laughing at her wee face putting him in his place. One December, when I was singing 'Oh Holy Night' with him playing the organ in our living room, he suggested, 'Why don't you sing it with me at Mass, Pandy?' and we got excited about it and practised every day. When Christmas morning arrived, though, I was suddenly crying scared. So close to the reality of it now ... Envisaging myself by him on the organ above the whole church, floating exposed on the balcony and all of the parish below listening ... Neighbours and friends and Christmas dolls ... The turning heads, the ears, the coughing in the echoing quiet ... The solemn pause of the bent and listening priest ... I couldn't do it. I have a vague recollection of being comforted by Mammy before she broke the news to Daddy. There was no real persuasion. I was ever so gently let off the hook. But I knew he was disappointed. It would have been a beautiful moment for him, I think now, when I imagine myself someday with my own child, and he did express that lovingly in a Baa way, over the years.

He went ahead of us to prepare and we followed on and joined the congregation.

When he began to play the introductory notes of 'Oh Holy Night', then by himself up there and me sitting below in a pew with Mammy, Jim, Sharon and Caroline, my heart started to beat as if there was yet another me up there with him, inhaling before I sing. But no voice, of course. It came and it went. And I was the only one that heard my heart beat for what might have been. I regretted it. And I am sorry now, today, because it would have been beautiful for me too, to sing with my daddy.

* * *

If a place is given such solemnity and gravity as the church is … if it's a very serious place, then it is near impossible for me not to laugh, to this day. But that was a gift from Mammy, too.

I am by the open grave of our next-door neighbour, Jack … His coffin is being lowered into the earth so slowly and so very carefully. All bent and reverent, we stand around and pray. And the rain it falls like tears. He is below now, in his eternal resting place, when they throw in a purple, pillowed … a purple, pillowed … body bag!!

'It's Bessie!' I thought, appropriately horrified (his wife who had predeceased him) and nudged and whispered to Mum …

'How come they just fling Bessie in like that, Mammy? That's not fair!' She shook with laughter at the graveside, hiding her face in her hands, and friends consoled her for being so upset.

Another time playing in church with my friend Sonia … I was up in one of the sculpted holy scenes, God forgive me, when an old lady came in to pray. There was no escape other than to join my hands in prayer and stand still as a statue beside Joseph. She prayed on. Didn't seem to wonder what a twelve-year-old girl in a school uniform had to do with Bethlehem.

Student exchange programme … Return fluent in Aramaic.

Having admitted that, though, I was kind of a holy child really … I loved – I still love – the hymns. 'Be Not Afraid',

'Here I Am, Lord', 'Walk in the Light', 'On Eagle's Wings', 'Abide with Me', 'Take Our Bread', 'How Great Thou Art' … I love the hope that they sing.

'Lord of the Dance' frightened me at Easter time, though …

I danced on a Friday when the sky turned black
It's hard to dance with the devil on your back
They whipped and they stripped
And they hung me on high
And left me there on the cross to die …

My children sang it with their school this Easter, I noticed, though it is a non-denominational school in London. Scary words, happy tune. They didn't seem fazed. The horror not real enough yet; long may that last. Strange seeing young, happy faces singing these words.

I prayed before bed every night in a superstitious and strict order … Opening the set with 'Oh my God you love me' and finishing with 'Oh angel of God my guardian dear' (there was rarely an encore) … It troubled me a little that they were all about blessing me through the day, so sometimes I'd substitute 'night', just so God would be clear. Another time, realising to myself that the prayers, having been learned off by heart, had lost their immediate meaning and truth, and that I drifted off helplessly reciting them, I altered them … A little shake-up … keep you on your toes … knees …

Our Father, who art in heaven
May thy name be kept holy …

And that has brought me back into the double bed with Caroline, and Mammy and Daddy at the door, the hall light illuminating them in golden silhouettes. I remember them saying 'Goodbye' and I would cry before the door shut: 'Say night night!' …

I must have had an innate fear of goodbye. Actually, maybe we all do. Maybe it's not a fear, but a presentiment.

If I still couldn't sleep after my prayers, my God blesses and the night nights, I would roll my head on the pillow from left to right and chant 'Mammy Daddy Daddy Mammy Daddy Mammy Mammy Daddy' over and over again. I had to mix them up in that way so neither was said more or continually take the lead and thus be favoured, but still it was very hard worrying about that. Of course, dizzy as I'd end up with all that head-rolling, conscious equality and self-hypnosis, I would roll off the precipice eventually into dreams.

Poor Caroline.

Have you ever tried to make your side of the bed, by the way? Caroline could do that. Perfect, down-the-middle neat with a one-eyed teddy bear named Tony on her pillow. Beside the aftermath of a tornado … I'd say making the whole bed was easier but what point would that make …

Jean Cried at Movies, Adverts and Soap Operas

That she was proportionately vocal when sneaked up on by a baddie is questionable. And when she didn't sit down and watch with us, preferring to watch the chicken turn gradually from stark naked to clothed and sit glorious and resplendent in the new NEFF oven they had purchased, she'd say:

'Look, Gerry, I'm just delighted with it!'

(The very same 'delighted!' she would later be, watching the rug that Caroline and Frank bought her and Daddy in India grow lush on our Dundalk living-room floor.)

When she did not sit down with us being otherwise kitchen-distracted, she would drive you demented or to bed, calling in every ten minutes:

'What happened?'

Or:

'Who's that?'

The tears rolled yearly down her cheeks watching *Gone with the Wind* and she'd laugh open-mouthed as if splashed in the eyes while she cried and we watched her. I also have a suspicion that she quietly thought Daddy a bit Irish Catholic uptight, not letting us watch *Dallas* or *Dynasty* or *The Colbys* or look at the cover of Prince's *Lovesexy* or the lyrics(!!) of Prince's *Lovesexy* …

She loved to cook, though she 'couldn't even boil an egg' when they got married, and there is the legend of the stubbornly rigor mortis turkey she'd had in the oven for twelve hours of Christmas one year (an early attempt to domestically woo James and Alice). But that is not the Mammy I knew … This is she …

The baking at Christmas. The smells, bags the bowl, the spatula, the serrated knife, I don't care, I want it, I am willing to bleed for it … Dundee cake batter. Up on chairs by her and the Kenwood chef spinning around singing and overcome as we were with the festive season and its aromatic cheer. Her roast potatoes, her salad sandwiches, her chicken sandwiches – her chicken soup! – her cole-slaw, her shepherd's pie (cottage pie, really … we Irish seem to prefer the name 'shepherd's', though of course we know well that beef has nothing to do with sheep). Her stews in the winter … Jim would eat two huge bowls with a whole, fresh, delivered-by-the-bread-man McCann's sliced pan and a glass of milk …

(I made 'Mammy's Irish Stew' the other day having thought of this … and our Filipino mother's help, Raquel, said with genuine kindness as I served her and her daughter:

'Don't mind, ma'am. We eat anything.'

She lay me down and massaged me this morning to ease my sick feeling and couldn't see me smile into the pillow …

She has my mother's hands.)

* * *

Mum answered the call of the blackbird from her kitchen window, like I can't help but do now. It is the only bird song I know, however. But Jean knew all the songs. She could name that tune in one. So Dad bought her a bird book, a pair of binoculars and a bird feeder, which hangs there still on the rhododendron over the rockery. (A mammy herself, that tree. She has two babies in the front.) And in the days where water giggled and flowed over those rocks and Jodie the bear-dog pranced about (he was a Border collie Mum brought home one day, much to Dad's displeasure … short-lived displeasure, as of course she knew it would be … She watched the seduction through the kitchen window. Gerry seated on those rocks. A black-and-white fur-ball at his feet, looking up at him in a silent, dog-to-man face-off … the picture of a landslide victory), there was a clematis weaving through the arch of a trellis and the flowers that hung from it were like vivid pink jewels of Eden. Their long, mower-lined garden was a thoroughfare of evergreens to lead you to the pink dream of a cherry tree when in blossom, and a crab apple tree. In the beds there were pansies, primroses and optimistic daffodils: my favourite flower, which I seemed to witness shivering and freezing yearly, through that window, almost as soon as they'd awoken to shine … Got to admire them for coming out at all, I think.

And they have the most beautiful smell … of hope.

Ah, but there's no hope beyond the cherry tree because that was far away to me. And it was the dark and ominous end of another's garden where my own mysterious bad boy Boo Radley, bowl-haired, tricycle-riding Damien Omen, lived.

He threw rocks at my swimsuited back one day and set the stinging bees on me ... I think. I passed him a few winters ago walking down the hill of Árd Easmuinn and thought, as we are grown up now, that I'd say hello ... He didn't respond, didn't look at me, just walked on by and when I gave up on my stupefied watch of his boy-man person getting smaller down the hill, and turned to continue, I was hit by a snowball in the back ...

For old times' sake.

I gave a bunch of dandelions to my teacher once, not realising, of course, that they were weeds. I had heard the rumour, though, that they made you pee the bed. Not there as well, I thought. We made daisy chains and proffered our chins for the do-you-like-butter buttercups test. And there was a vegetable patch with cabbage, lettuce leaves and rhubarb growing ... And the warm, ripe Irish tomatoes tang in the glasshouse behind this patch, which made your eyes water when you walked in and were engulfed in the foreign humidity and the zinging smell of greenhouse life ...

Yes ... Jean had green fingers beneath an earth-worn oven glove.

She made clothes upstairs on her Singer sewing machine, too ... three jumpsuits with moonstone pop buttons in different materials for Sharon, Caroline and

60

me. Mine was a little see-through when the wind hit me, I noticed. So I put on one of Sharon's bras, got on my bicycle and cycled fast down the hill of our road … I put my hands in my pockets for further grown-up, casual, bike-gliding cool and fell over like an armless skittle. Now let that be a lesson to you.

She made Jim's Communion suit, too: wee navy shorts and a striped waistcoat over a navy blue polo neck. He looks mortified beside her in the photograph. And she is wearing a beautiful outfit she also made … Sharon and I, both, have worn it since … A black, sleeveless, slim wool dress, with a high neck and a band of glittering silver beneath a pink-satin-lined black cape. She entered it in a fashion competition before we were born and was 'robbed', they said, of first place.

She also made Caroline's and my confirmation dresses. The same drop-waisted, cup-sleeved pattern but again in different materials, which she let us choose ourselves from the selection in Dearey's Drapery on Clanbrassil Street. Caroline's was summer peach cotton, which she wore with a white brimmed hat and silk peach ribbon and a pair of white dainty shoes. She even had a wee white handbag … Lady Diana is here and she is only beautiful. I, as you probably imagine at this point, did not choose colours appropriate to this religious and solemn occasion and I think it's remarkable now that Mum ever allowed me. Lovely, really, and loving, allowing me an early expression of individuality even though she must have seen … Letting the baby go a little because she is twelve. But there's no getting away from it: the Holy Spirit descended upon a holy show the day I was confirmed. He probably ascended right back up again, in fact, as soon as He caught sight of me, and called an emergency meeting with the other blessed Two. The Twinity.

It was black with small white flowers, red-painted shoes, black nylons (honestly), a red hat with a black-and-red polka-dot ribbon. And la pièce de résistance … a widow's black netting over my eyes. Unsurprisingly the teacher did not want me in the class photo. She tried to hide the siren in the back. But there's charcoal staining the pastels like a naughty thumbprint and you just can't rub me out.

There are clothes of Gerard's in a crumpled brown Dunnes paper bag in the cupboard above her wardrobe. A suit she made him. A beige wool blazer with round brown buttons. Trousers and shorts to match. There's a green polo-neck jumper that he is wearing with those shorts in a photo I've seen of him sitting between Mum and Jim on a blanket on the front lawn. He faces the camera in one of these photos, but in another he is the only one looking away. He is looking behind him towards our next-door neighbour's house. To his friend Brian, maybe. That is chilling to think of now. I held his worn brown Clarks shoes in my hands. And I smelled the striped T-shirt that would've been close to his body. God love them. Mammy, Daddy and Jim.

Mum also helped us all with our knitting and sewing for school. They don't teach that anymore. I see the checked blue tacking square and now I hear the sound of her needles knitting … very easy and fast. It was too obvious when she had done a few rows for us, as those beautiful smooth rows of plain and purl invariably led to a disturbing section of holes. Crazy golf. Making you wonder, had the knitter suddenly suffered a stroke?

I knitted my husband a scarf for Christmas one year. I still don't know how to ensure the sides don't curl in, though. And as he is tall, I overdid it on the length a bit. He is six foot two and it curls round his neck to drape – no, to drip, really – down to the floor and curl once more, in a grand finale, by his shoes. Like two pet animals sleeping at the feet of their master. It was a very Dickens Christmas.

'Pandy' by Gerry Corr

Dinner done
Time for some fun
So we watched TV
Little Pandy and me

Perched high on my knee
Little eyes to see
Old friends on screen
So many there's been!

Pugh, Pugh, Barney McGrew
Cuthbert, Dibble, Grub
Captain Flack and Barleymow
PC Copper and Aunt Flo

Now back at work
Old nostrils perk up
Is it horse manure?
I'm really not sure!
So slow to perceive
You'll never believe ...
She peed on my knee
While we watched TV!

Goody Goody
Yum Yummmmmm!

Oh I loved *The Goodies*! Bearded men were always a fave, as Daddy had a beard. I cried when he considered shaving it, so he didn't. Years later, in a Santa Monica hotel, Jim and I shaved his head over the bath and freed him from a comb-over and 'the tyranny of hairspray'.

Gerry Says No!

Thank you, Andrea and Jim. It's hard to be convincingly angry when the wind is lifting your hair like a lid and you racing up the road for twelve o'clock Mass ...

Not the Nine O'Clock News, Spitting Image, Fawlty Towers, Blackadder, The Kenny Everett Show ...

'It's all done in the best posssssssible taste!'

Dallas ... 'They're all rolling in and out of bed with each other. Turn over!'

(Pam's finding rolling a little painful today, sorry.)

Terry Wogan's *Blankety Blank* chequebook and pen!

Les Dawson, the best bum-noting entertainer.

And I confess, though I hardly need to now (it's par for the Corrs ... ba-dum) ...

The Benny Hill Show.

Top of the Pops was a call to prayer, though.

Time for a quick commercial break.

(Ah, bloomin' ads.)

Let's ask our expert, Neill ...

You mean which bleach kills germs longest in the lavatory?

Oh, cock your head to the right on the first revealing syllable and tell me, Neill ... please?

It's Vortex.

Oh, so satisfying! Thank you, Neill. And by the way ... It looks to me like someone's been using Ariel on their white coat ...

Things that 'appen te ma bridal gowns. Mud on the emmm, or even ...

Persil?

Ahhhh, Mummmm!

Don't tell me ...

BOLD 3! (Slam the box down on the counter, why don't ye! Bold as Brasso, you are!)

Now hands that do dishes can feel soft as your face, with mild green ... (altogether now)

Fairy Liquid.

Irish Permanent ... Come on, Grandad, sure you haven't said a word all evening and us comatosed watching RTÉ One beside you ... He joined in:

The people's choice ... (Run before we explode, Caroline.)

Mammies by the sink.

Mammies Shake n' Vac-ing.

Mammies and babies' bums.

Milk of magnesia?

That's the one.

Imperial Leather.

Clinic shampoo.

Timotei, tell me …

I could look like you?

Could you put the dinner on? I'll be home in twenty minutes.

Bedeholymuckintiggersamuckholy! Is that a woman telling a man to cook the tea??!!

Haha says you … very clever!

I loved the smell of the heating on in the winter. The switch on the wall above the organ, and it omming to a start. The radiators cracking their knuckles and 'All right, so'ing.

Oh Mum is on the couch and now I'm laughing. She would sit … lie … recline, in a blue quilted sleeping bag. Whatever she had been wearing on her bottom half, draped over the back of it.

I was a teenage, smiling Curehead (Stop that, you're supposed to be depressed), with my similar alternative friends, in the kitchen ('Mm, do you like The Smiths more than The Cure?) when a slow shuffle-hop sound distracts me and here's Mammy hopping past, on her way to the bathroom. Losing the sack race in a fit of the giggles.

'Pick up your jeans, Andrea!' she splutters.

My jeans??!!

We holidayed every July in Skerries and it smells to me now of rashers and the sunny peaches outside O'Neill's corner shop …

A fruit auditorium

Perusing me.

Mm, not sure …

There's a lot of cuts on her knees.

I don't need to investigate further.

This one is bruised.

Her??

I thought her a gypsy boy.

Well I don't mind …

There's a box of Tayto in the back room of our chalet.

(Suck them beside Daddy; he's grumbling with the noise.)

It's funny how a musician-parented family such as we were, in a red Toyota Hiace van (our transport had also become their trailer for the gear), was perceived. Something we were happily unaware of, till a Skerries friend of Sharon's came home with us to stay.

As we slowed down the hill of Árd Easmuinn, the van indicating left, she showed genuine shock when we were moving up the drive of a middle-class, two-storey house.

Kids sang 'Born on a Dual Carriageway' to me there, and I sang along. Why not? That's a good song.

Irish Snobbery. A contradiction in terms.

There was a time when Mum got our sizes wrong when buying our school tights.

Did you keep the receipt, Mrs?

Of course I did, as always ...

Ah but I wouldn't want to put a man's brain in a woman's head now, would I, haha, he said.

Ah sure how would it fit, tell me? Ye stupo!

Oh how we laughed.

Anyway, I got so tired of pulling them up at home that I got used to walking around, a shackled convict on house arrest, after school. Then one day in the cookery kitchen, I was practising making porridge, stirring away goodo, when a friend exclaimed ...

'Andrea, your tights!'

I had a very strange tolerance of discomfort, it seems. Caroline scratching her head off, her face, and all getting involved while I continued on happily without even the tickle of an itch. I, of course, was found to be 'crawling' when she had on board a solitary lodger ... A bachelor, methinks, already on his way out. There was a suicidal bachelor in her attic room. Driving her cuckoo. Yes. That was it. Was nit? *Try not to scratch.*

Oh she was so good though, Mum. Over me so carefully, so diligently, gently, with that dreaded fine-tooth

71

comb (it is not a fine experience) way past bedtime, so I would not have the horribly less fine experience later when the community fled the poison. She'd arrest and handcuff as many as she could before I'd ever experience that.

I think it's unfair how much mums do with all of their love and how much love and comradeship dads get. How I loved horsey-back when he'd had a few. Me giddy and weakening her silent fight. (Her face is finding this 'SLTH' methinks ... mmmm slightly less than hilarious ...)

But now I am a mum of two. I have a girl comeuppance and a boy comeuppance. And maybe it is absolutely fair. It is all that I could want, anyway.

She tried to lock Daddy out once, they told me … Sliding the latch in the kitchen back door and giving out under her breath. I watched her silently and then proceeded to drag a chair to the door, stood up on it and unlatched it as definitively as she had latched it. I see you and I raise you, Mammy. I turned to her then, still up on the chair maintaining the authority this newfound height brought me, and I gave her a look that told her not to even think about locking my daddy out. She obeyed, defeated by the indignant stance of a five-year-old, and they laughed about it later.

'You only see the fight, Pandy. You don't see the making up.'

But my daddy was often to be found in the doghouse with a bachelor friend of his, John, who had 'no responsibilities, no wife and children to go home to'. One Friday night, having gone on the lash together after work, Daddy and John swayed home together. Mammy made them a curry so hot that John bawled and roared over the windowed oval table. Reflected in it, a rabid and grizzly bear seated with a big white tea-towel bib around his neck. His entire being boiling … like a lobster screeching red from the scalding water …

'JEAN!!! ARGHHHHHHHHHH!!!'

She left the room and laughed. That'll learn ye.

Frustrated again one evening in front of the fire, the *Irish Times* flick-flicking, coughing 'Ahem' to gape in front of her face … shaking shuddering with the weight of the serious, frowning Irishman issues it contained, she lit a match and burned it from the middle seam up, Daddy's stunned face appearing behind the rising flame, his hands still holding either side.

Aynsley China and boxes of 'All because the lady … forgives?' Milk Tray.

They were the 'Baa sorry Jean' peace offerings and the 'making up' that I did see.

On Valentine's Day she would check the *Irish Times* and smile when she spotted the anonymous riddle meant only for her. This one I remember …

Dinner and wine
Brown eyes benign
Nellies sublime
Oh creature divine
How hungry I'm …

They, unlike us today, spent very few nights apart … So few, in fact, that I remember them. There are gifts of stained-glass pagodas from the market in Covent Garden where he went with Jim. A trip to the music shops of London, I'd say. They shelter the dust in the old overripe glasshouse now. Or a visit to his best friend and tennis partner Gerry Crosby, or to his brother Willy, in Dublin. Mum then would seem to have waited eagerly for his phone call like a debutante, for she would cry, 'That's Gerry!' when the phone rang. And she would dress up and have Jodie, shining healthy, to wait for him off the train that came in across our road. Each of them made the

74

other more beautiful, he thought. You could feel then, too, an excitement between them. A shy, smiling strangeness. And I get a glimpse of the two of them independent of us, back in the Fiat 500 on the corner of McSwiney Street.

'Be Careful What You Wish For' for Mum

Head dishevelled like I'm Einstein
In a hurricane of fury
I don't remember the last time
I woke up naturally
I'm a coffee addict double buggy pushin speed walker
Happy hour means a whole lot more to me
So this is what it's like
Flung from one day to the next
Try to get the balance right
But I haven't got it yet
Be careful what you wish for

You know I wouldn't have it
Any other way
I just remembered
It's my birthday today
So I'll have burnt toast
And you can eat up all my cake
I didn't wanna know how old I was anyway ...

F our years when you are a child is a big age difference, ten huge … and one year is practically none, therefore my playing memories are Caroline's. She is almost always with me in them. We were 'the children' of the house and Jim and Sharon were grown up, even when they weren't. That's why Caroline is my twin twister. And why I was born with one ready-made best friend and two mothers. She was naive to my cunning and it made me laugh all day long, every day long. I was absolutely free of worry. She was not. It was great.

'Caroline, will we steal a biscuit?'

'OK, let's.'

So we would steal a custard cream each. I would pretend to eat mine while, unwittingly, she devoured hers. Then I would put mine back.

God! I'm laughing here but this is awful!

You'll be surprised to hear that I didn't do this just once.

But how we entertained ourselves and each other every day. The two of us. Wrapping the duvets around our bodies and tying a belt around our waists to emerge adorned in Victorian dresses. We would take a walk of the room, how better to show off our figures, and we would drink from silver goblets. Whoever then was queen would recline on the sofa and be fanned and fed grapes by the other. We would play mammies and babies. She the mammy and me the baby. And I would remind her frequently with my eyes closed (Ah look … the little curly baby) to say, 'Shhh, the baby's asleep.' We would do the slow silent drift, two ghosts in Muppets nightdresses, from our bed back to the living room, and linger and float behind the corner, spying on the TV … circling closer and secretly watching with them, until we were spotted and made to flee.

'But we haven't had our cereal!'

Bathtime was a complete laugh. We simmered together to a slow, steady boil in the bubbles before we exploded out, newborn down the stairs, into the living room for the unannounced evening performance of giddy bums.

(Bare bums are just funny. Always were and always will be.)

Betimes, she, the twinkle-toed ballerina, would pirouette gracefully into the living room and I would enter abruptly and with gravitas, her intimidatingly handsome danseur, in school tights with tennis balls stuffed down them.

(They are funny too.)

She was subtle. I was not. Green eyeshadow and red lipstick. The whole bold and dirty face in carnival colour, to her Lady Diana. She would have a modest bosom, econ-omising on the toilet-roll padding, and I would have, well … just … huge … gigantic … Forget about the toilet-roll padding, I'm all in with facecloths or clothes or blankets or, if handy – happy days! – balloons.

Oh, that reminds me: we used to laugh at the sound of a word. Particularly when Mammy said it.

My breasts.

Breasts.

Say it? It is funny, isn't it?

Breasts.

Yes. It is.

'Twisters'

Pillowcase sledging
Down the stairs
Tennis balls in tights
Living room ballet
Her rollers heat

She's ready to bounce
The night
Her slips
Our long hair
Dolly tissue silhouette
Lipstick I blush
My smile
Outran my mouth
The yucca plant
The skeeting gun
Play tears
Play tumble down

After bath
Our towel capes
They flee the crib tonight
Victorian dresses
Heaven blessed
Our world
No kryptonite

I miss that home.

Music

Dad, as well as working in payroll for the ESB for forty years, was a musician. A keyboard player and an organist, he played various gigs, weddings, funerals and pubs around Louth. He used to joke – self-deprecatingly, yet, I believe, sincerely – 'If only my talent were on a par with my passion.' He found himself in need of a singer and, such were the times that they lived in, failed to look to his wife, likely peeling potatoes at the kitchen sink.

'I'm doing it,' she said, matter of fact and, ahead of her time, that's what she became … the singer of The Sound Affair.

Their first gig was brutal, they have told us. After it was over, a member of the audience remarked:

'No harm to yiz, but youse are the worst band I've ever seen.'

But on the way home in the car, Mammy said to Daddy, 'I just love it.'

And so they played for twenty years. Got a lot better than that first fateful night and built up quite a following.

Now that I'm a mother I think about what an important release this must have been for her. An expression of herself beyond us and Dad. Something so few women got back then. The person in the mirror she looked up to as she put rollers in her hair and put on her make-up. Her own unique and secret truth that she found in the words she sang.

And there was colour in her wardrobe then. Her stage clothes and shoes. Someone that she was that I don't have full access to.

I think there may have been an underlying fear in Ireland that if a woman, never mind a mother, was exposed in the open, they just may be stolen or even fly away (ah ... 'Don't be stolen' is something Mum and Dad used to say to each other ...) Actually, when I think about it, this must still be a factor when we think of the resistance to women having free choice about their own bodies. Sure we can't be trusted of course. We're not up to 'the run of ourselves' and may lose it …

You don't think of this when you watch your mother as a child. But you do when you're cooking 'pasgetty' for your children's packed lunch in the morning. The morning after you played London's O2. And a proper Irish house-wife of my mother's era would never be out and exposed like that. It was made a little more permissible alongside her husband, I imagine.

I think I felt the danger once. When I hear 'Love Me Tender' I see the arm of a fellow musician steal over her shoulder to teach her to play it on guitar.

Yes, I suppose it may put the whole house at risk.

Let's sacrifice the woman and all will be well.

This …

… is the scene we grew up in. A home immersed in music. The radio always on. The weekly charts like Mass. The stereo set to record. The original illegal downloads.

'Quick, quick, get it!!' Mum would shout from the kitchen and whoever was there would run, frantic not to miss the first line, as this was about transcribing the lyrics for the lyric book. This is what they would learn, rehearse and play in The Coachman's Inn, The Muirhevna Inn, one of the many inns, the following weekend. Thursday through Sunday.

She had an ear for what would be a hit. They performed 'Don't Cry for Me Argentina' weeks before it was in the Top Ten. Indeed, this was often where people heard what were to become their favourite songs for the very first time. ABBA, the Eagles, the Carpenters, Simon and Garfunkel, Roy Orbison.

She is coming alive as I write. Maybe she really did come alive in this time. What music did for her, what it awoke in her? It is a physical blooming in front of my closed eyes now.

And maybe I did feel the physical change in her, and just maybe this is a memory, too. From 1974 (you see, I was hiding there, that brutal first gig that hooked her) through the 80s, into the 90s when they, oh so reluctantly, surrendered. The lugging in and out of the gear had gotten too much for them. Not the music. Never the music. So on a bittersweet happy new year, The Sound Affair was over.

There are not many vivid evenings when we got to watch The Sound Affair, at home being babysat most of the time and a pub being 'no place for children'. I am around for her preparations, though. The smell of Friar's Balsam. Her head beneath a tea towel inhaling the vapour from a bowl at the kitchen table. Olbas oil on her pillow. A singer's paraphernalia in her mammy handbag. Lozenges and Sinex sticks. Rehearsals and late-afternoon naps for them both before they left for 'Mammy and Daddy's Sing'.

Our weekend habits told the story, too, of our working musician parents. Our house rose late, unlike our neighbours. Kept its eyes closed way into morning with drawn curtains. And the glass milk bottles stood still and waiting at the front door. The sun shining directly on their silver-and-red foil tops. Early bird-pecked for the cream.

You snooze, you lose.

But we loved weekends. The lie-ins. They seemed so happy and relaxed, those late mornings, early afternoons. She would cook a big fry and we would all appear around the table at various stages. I'd say they retained the glow of the previous night's gig and felt good. And maybe they both stood outside of themselves, on those mornings after. Looked through the kitchen window and saw in there that they had it all. Just about. I think I recognise that feeling now.

There is one night in The Coachman's Inn with our Nanna Lizzy I vaguely recall when I try. But all I seem to have retained is the taste of the Coke and peanuts that I was really there for.

Or maybe I absorbed how poor Nanna felt, those ghostly days in her surprised presence. For she was then surfing the skipping record, and we were indeed minding her.

It started in her early sixties and at this stage she was already looking like she had just gotten the worst fright. Horror-stricken. Her white hair stood up perpetually from her hypnotic self-soothing. The continuous and purposeful upward stroke of her long bony hand through the hair above her anxious brow. Again and again and again. Slowly but surely, she was rubbing herself out.

It is awful, Alzheimer's disease, even to the eyes of a child. To witness the slow live fade-out of a loved human being. To see Mum over her own mother's bed, holding a cold and unresponsive hand. Reaching towards a lifeless expression, for eyes to engage and see again. For one elusive moment of lucidity. Telling her who she, her daughter, was …

'Mammy, it's me … Jean.'

But sometimes in life, it seems, disease can arrive with a comic introduction. If you don't laugh you'll cry.

She boiled a head of lettuce. That's how it first showed itself. And they all laughed, she included, knowing so little of what was coming. Of who …

'Where's yours, Jean? Paddy, Paddy, Paddy. The dog, the dog, the dog …'

The sad truth is that I was too young to have met who Lizzy really was or who she had ever, if only for too short a time, been.

I can smell the horses outside The Coachman's and the fat of grilled sirloin steak, fried onion rings and the frost of the forbidden night-time … an anniversary of theirs … when he softened enough in the familial smiling wine hug of it all for her to approach the ear-piercing subject.

A roaring success. Sharon had green studs, Caroline blue, and me … danger dizzy red.

S ometimes I imagine we clocked up many of Gladwell's 'ten thousand hours' in the very air we breathed in that house. And the inevitability of it all is like a carnival, slowly but surely winding its way towards us. The wind carrying the whisper of it every now and then. Because all the while we were growing. One brother to three sisters in a border town. And I see it all as a film reel turns, fast-forwards and flickers to a stop. Through the pebble-dash snow the pictures emerge and slow, and the tastes are in my mouth ...

Cucumber and cheese
On a cocktail stick
Banana sandwiches
Orange splits
The apple swung with the money in
Dad held to help me keep
Mum's apple tart
The barn braic
God bless before you sleep
We'll have Jean's mince pies

And Oh Holy Nights
Say the ghosts of the settee
Rhubarb dreams
And cut grass
And pencil on my hands
Skinny legs, a runny nose,
Short hair for boy or girl ...

Jim has perfect pitch, though he allows for a semitone sharp. For that was the persistent tuning of Grandad's black piano upstairs. And he was the trailblazer. Being the eldest, he pushed the merry-go-round. He was always mouth-drumming or knee-drumming or head-drumming. An all-the-toms fill would alert us to his arrival – if we had managed to miss the unique sound only he made when turning the handle of the kitchen door. It just was so definitive. No question. This door shall open! Or indeed the door left open. Cue Gerry:

'Could you shut the bloody dooooooor!' Musical in itself, how Gerry voiced this. It started low and rose both in tone and volume and he danced on the word 'bloody' before he crescendoed and held 'doooooor' on the money note. Immersed in music, we were.

Jim's bedroom housed the piano. And the high, out-of-reach (you'd think) shelves of his mahogany wardrobe held his remote-control helicopter and his train set. Always my first port of call when on the best side of sick. Still off school in a stolen day alone in the house and roaming free in my nightgown.

We were all taught to play that piano from the age of six. So when I peer into that room with its purple walls, one of us is always there.

For Sharon's practical exam in her Music Leaving Cert she played a piano piece she had composed herself. It was haunting and beautiful. She is there playing that now in my mind's eye, in our bottle-green St Louis school uniform. And she loved to play Erik Satie. There's something about the touch of her hand on the keys still. Something romantic.

And of course, as there is only fourteen months between Caroline and myself, we shared – as we did everything else – what became known as the 'terrifying piano lessons'.

I never could quite decide which was best for me, to go first or second. For she was the golden child. Fingers tinkling away while I nervously waited on the bed, sucking my thumb. Actually seeing the smile of pride on the back of his head. In retrospect … no argument. Go first, Andrea.

Daddy would grumble behind me, 'Ach, fingering,' while I tried to swap my thumb for my baby finger. Small hands knotting and twisting the Beethoven.

Caroline, God love her, didn't enjoy this either. Every single week she would plead with me,

'Andrea, you need to practise your piano. It's Monday … lesson on Thursday.' And every week, Wednesday would arrive and I'd have been too busy to practise, so I would learn what she now played perfectly by frenzied ear and thus not have a clue where my fingers should go. I would run out of fingers every second bar.

It's like our nanna, who one day I saw relentlessly trying to walk through the glass in the sliding doors. Again and again and again. Poor Lizzy Blee.

But somewhere I never needed reminding to be was the 'bumping' chair by the record player, corner of the living room, by the window. On the contrary, I needed to be pulled off it to go to school in the mornings and to bed at night.

I must pause here and define bumping.

To bump … While seated normally on an upright, cushion-backed armchair, one rocks back and forth to the rhythm of the music, hitting the chair back, with one's own back, on the downbeat (*Corrs Dictionary*, circa 1980).

91

We all bumped to various degrees (Gerard included) but I was the champion bumper. My absolute favourite pastime as a child. I'd sing with the singers and be the characters in these three-minute stories. More than a little bit disconcerting to Dad's ear, hearing his ten-year-old sing 'Darling Nikki'.

So if I really am the original loser, or indeed 'danger dizzy', as Jim named me, it is due to the fact that the areas in my brain assigned to hold on to keys, credit cards, phones, etc., have been burgled and colonised by words. There are lyrics loitering there from before I was born, claiming squatters' rights. (Ah! Mum wasn't the only one hooked!)

I remember a painter working in the house, kindly asking me to stop playing 'River Road', and a friend of Sharon's who came to stay, not so kindly, to stop playing 'There Must Be an Angel'. But not once did Mum or Dad tell me to stop. It was indeed very rare for them to tell me to turn it down and now I see the wonder of that. I'd say it was nearly more annoying for them when I had the headphones on, while they watched *Panorama* or Daddy's 'aul' news', than when it was blaring. The music bleeding through my headphones and the whining springs of a near-extinct, beloved bumping chair.

But we were all so affected by songs.

Jim little more than a toddler, in tears begging Daddy 'Don't play "Daddy Boy"' ("Danny Boy"). And this boy with all the talent Daddy's passion yearned for, would go on to help them and even play with The Sound Affair a few times. So easy was it for him to listen once and write down the chords of every new song they were learning. Something that was painstaking for Daddy was so natural for him. As if his ears were born fluent in music.

Jim saved up or was helped (I'd say more often helped because how could you not help when you have been known yourself to appear home delighted with a synthesiser instead of a new vacuum cleaner …) and he bought a TASCAM 244 Portastudio. Then he was up there recording. His head nodding in headphones. His knobble-knuckled fingers playing basslines, snares, kicks, high-hats, toms, padded strings, piano and brass (very questionable … should be banned) all on a keyboard, rocking back and forth all the time, his expression intense. I have seen a computer screen reflected in his glasses so often that it now appears to me always there. It was all he wanted to spend his time doing back then. There were early songs I really loved and would bump to when he'd let me have the tape he'd made (can't scratch it but can wear it out … spooly mess … Run!). I could sing them still. He had disco lights in there that flashed red, amber and purple on the walls and hopped to the music and sometimes he would amplify his voice and an 'Andreaaaaaa!' would descend on me from nowhere …

Like God had caught me doing what I shouldn't be.

And we followed him through the years, the fashions, the genres.

Mod-dancing through the awkward cool pain of adolescence.

Ska, punk, pop …

Pop held on to him though and still does, I believe. Melody. The beautiful chords he writes that make my heart swell, lose a breath, inspire … His were the records I bumped into skipping, into scratched. When I hear these songs now I still sing the skips; they repeat in my head like a malfunctioning robot and Nanna's hitting the glass again. These will never be the grooves the artist intended.

Nik Kershaw, The Human League, Kraftwerk, Heaven 17, The Police …

In a box in the attic now.

There's a parallel house
And another Blackrock
A parallel family
Three girls and a boy
But the dad is the singer
Two brothers the band
A minor detail now
We never know where we'll land ...

John Meets a Family Band

The clever lunacy of it all. How random yet fated. Because it seems to me now that John Hughes was always to be the fifth Corr.

He was a singer and songwriter, in a band with his brother. They made the Billboard Hot 100 but it all fell apart. They fell apart.

And he was out on his own.

Jim at this point was a session musician, keyboards and guitar, with an 8-track recording studio. They met through mutual friends and worked together, recording and producing a couple of John's songs.

In the meantime, Alan Parker was coming to Dublin to begin open casting for the film *The Commitments*. And John's childhood friend, Ros Hubbard, was casting with John himself, co-ordinating all the band and music auditions. For The Commitments were to be a real band. Real singers and musicians. He advised Jim to audition. Jim asked to bring along his three sisters. And our family became a band.

Big-haired, blushing, caught between bunny-in-the-headlights shy and divadom, we performed 'Knock on Wood' and 'I Don't Go for That'. No drums, no violin, no guitar. An arm-swinging, hip-swaying lead singer and three keyboard-playing backing vocalists.

And now our pivotal moment. Ros Hubbard to John: 'I'm gonna go out on a limb now, but John, you should manage this band; and Corrs, John should manage you.'

And somehow, it was absolutely right. No question. Of course.

Now another house
The back of the wall
Egg carton
Wall papered
Sound boothing
Us all
School uniformed girls
And bespectacled boy
And a Sandymount faithful
To Music, the Call

So we started to write and record in a house Jim rented in Mount Avenue, Dundalk, an area known as 'the back of the wall'. The very first offerings, Dad wrote lyrics into

Jim's keyboard melodies, like slotting shapes into a puzzle. 'I Feel Love' and 'Siog' (meaning Fairy Fort). If the song got beyond my range (well a song about fairies probably should, in all honesty), Jim speeded the track up and I soared like a chipmunk; or if indeed it got too low, as was 'Siog', he tried slowing me down down down, and there I was in the belly of a whale.

And it was pop as 90s pop could be. Brass-stabbed D50 explosive drama time. Hungry hands in desert sands (not Daddy any more, *mea culpa*). Out on my own, leave me alone.

But by this time John's wife, Marie 'de blonde', and their four kids had caught the bug. A virus that attacks the ears. You no longer hear the bad, and you're high on 'what's good about it'-itis.

And if you listened really carefully and turned the sound down, in those embryonic days, you may have heard the pleading lament of a neglected violin, leaking out of a case in Sharon's bedroom five minutes away.

John heard it.

'You play the violin, Sharon. Why aren't you playing it?'

Dundalk had been blessed with a talented teaching priest, Father McNally. And Sharon had grown up as one of his students. Reluctant at times … lessons on a Saturday don't do it for most teenagers, but doesn't it show you that sometimes it really is worthwhile for parents to insist. She travelled when she was around fifteen with the Irish Youth Orchestra, all the way to

Wallingford, Connecticut (can't believe I have remembered that. I can see it on the 'I heart Wallingford' T-shirt she wore home), and she visibly loved it … looked different when she came home, like she had a secret. And the awe and wonder grew a little more in me as I watched, still and always the baby.

Her training was classical, yes, but here comes our signature: with her classical bowing she wrote trad–pop riffs.

This grew wings, for like a zeitgeist in our own little world, traditional Irish music reached out to each of us. We all worked in our Auntie Lilian's pub, and the Thursday-night trad sessions were epic. The flute player from these sessions, Kevin Shields, taught me the tin whistle. And Caroline learned bodhrán through a videotape, believe it or not. I suppose that's today's YouTube lesson.

She also happened to have a drumming boyfriend at the time, and this is how she became 'The Drummer'. Her focus is ferocious. Paradiddling through Band-Aids and golf gloves, her girl hands blistered and her job corresponding with her black-and-white brain. Kick, snare, kick, snare.

We would walk together to Jim's rented house at the back of the wall, Sharon's violin swinging by her side, Caroline and myself still in our school uniforms. There were always cups of what I presume was old tea with maps of algae growing on their surface. Somehow it always reminds me of the aerial view of Los Angeles through the window of an aeroplane now. The skin on that cold milky tea. When cleaned (of course), I would have the baby cup (of course). We ate Toffypops, Wagon Wheels, Kimberleys, Mikados and Snowballs in an upstairs front room. A Müller Rice was seen as a healthy and sophisticated option. Carton sitting by Sharon's chair, its silver tongue curled and a licked happy spoon fallen by its side. There were torn orange curtains partially drawn on the squared sash windows that looked out either side onto a country road, stone walls and fields. If you wiped the condensation, that is, that ever lingered on the inside of those squares. (Oh, there's an earwig in the black mouldy damp corner! Where have all the earwigs gone? Are they endangered now? I never see them any more. #savetheearwig.) And speaking of insects, there was a spider in a web spanning one of the peeling wall corners, which Jim named Henry. We never managed to figure out whether Henry was alive or dead.

Just chillin' to the tunes, man. Spider on the wall rockumentary, if you will.

The room's walls were decorated with egg cartons and purple fruit trays to insulate the sound, and by the back window there was a stand and microphone adorned with a homemade pop shield of wire hanger and a stretched nude nylon tights leg.

Welcome to the recycled studio.

Black-and-grey flexes were strewn about along with random pieces of orange carpet (orange? Again?) liable to

send you tumbling onto the Superser (in winter you could smell the gas from it and three bars lit orange(!!) were never enough). Or worse, you'd stumble on the equipment and get tangled in the skeleton of a keyboard stand. Jim cradling his Precious above you, at war with a robot in the scrap. A surgeon's reflexes, he had.

(Knock knock.

Who's there?

Orange.

Orange who?

Orange ye glad I said orange again.)

This house was the gate lodge to an equestrian school and horses clippity-clopped by daily, but never at night thankfully, when we recorded vocals until the cusp of late and early. We all loved coming up with harmonies together. We still do. We can feel the resonance. A sort of buzz or phasing when we sing together. Something about the vocal cords being so similar and yet coming from four individuals. It seems to grow warm. I like to imagine it's the sound and vibration of the minutest differences, rather than the similarities.

Or maybe it is Gerard … The ghost in our machine …

I vividly remember returning after school one day to listen to what we had finished recording at 3 a.m. that morning, to hear it all absolutely synched together … absolutely in tune with each other and absolutely, woefully flat. My whole body reaches up when I remember it. My eyebrows, my shoulders … Up up up. To this day I much prefer sharp to flat. If you have to slide off-piste at all, that is.

Jim worked for hours while we did a lot of watching. Rocking on three wooden chairs facing him in his illuminated, blinking, beeping office of computers, keyboards, drum machines and guitars. A surgery, really. Dr Jim. The family doctor.

He really did a lot of work on these first demos, though. And it is true that a lot of what was recorded in that room made it onto our first record, or at the very least, was mimicked.

Sharon would pluck the beginnings of tunes on her violin and we would all hum melodies inspired by the sound. These melodies would often, unsurprisingly, sound similar.

The words were in the day and from … somewhere in the heart, yes, but it is also true that they were very much

101

straitjacketed in the rigid laws of rhyme in those nursery days, and the fit of their individual rhythms into the all-important melody was paramount. Often we repeated verses and I don't personally have the honest excuse that I heard from a young writer the other day: 'Because I really like that verse.' We treasured every moment of a six-minute middle eight (until Johnny broke the spell. Enough is enough) but we could halve a verse happily. Fewer words to write. To repeat.

I think it's true to say that we were moved and excited more by music than by words in those days. Today words almost do it all for me. Look at me now. Ha. Mutually exclusive they are not, though, nor will they ever be, and this is the song every songwriter is trying to write, I believe. When the music cuts your heart out describing the true meaning in the words. The blood and the beat. The pulse and the pain of the only human heart. That is when a song is truly worthy of its name, to me.

One day, walking to that house, Jim told me that he had itchy feet. I said:
    'Really, Jim? That's amazing. So are mine!'
    I did not know what he meant then, but I do now.
    And so backing vocals into the morning.
    Horizontal on the carpet.
    Roll a metre away from the Superser …
    And there's smoky frost in your words again.

And then school the next day … like the night before never was. But there was evidence and it built up slowly.

Forgiven, Not Forgotten was being born.

And now for the years that made the overnight success.

Blind, naive, bolstered faith. For this was never to be local. We were to 'rule the world', as Daddy would say.

'There will be a time when you will never be home,' John would say, like a missionary telling us,

'St Peter will indeed let you in!'

And underneath our collective, excited enthusiasm, I was, in honesty, terrified.

Because I loved home. I love feeling safe.

Demo tapes appeared on desks
Big black and white cheeked photos
While the ministry of serious walks
Transported insured ears
They chin scratched through showcases
And friend filled papered gigs
A cockney accent lingers
Too confident to feel
'I can't 'ear it. I just can't 'ear it'
To a word we'd never say
It echoed throughout London
Just like a big mistake.

We set up in the room across the hall from the studio, the room of terrors … I mean mirrors … where we would rehearse for TV shows and gigs, and we used Daddy's camcorder to record ourselves, watch back and endeavour to eliminate what no unsuspecting viewer sitting down to watch the telly of an evening should ever see. Sadly this wasn't foolproof, so I apologise for my spaghetti swinging arms. Miraculous I didn't knock over anything or anyone or just gather momentum with all that arm-swinging till I rotated and couldn't stop. Have to be carted off while the credits ran. A spinning flop. And I apologise on behalf of Caroline, who stared at you eerily while she played the keyboard, like Joey 'The Lips's mammy, till you felt shifty and uncomfortable there in your own chair, in your own house, innocently watching what should have been a lovely programme. Sharon calls herself a rosy-cheeked and wholesome dairy-maid taking a break from the milking to play her violin. Lovely girl. Jim was even rosy, when spotted.

It has been revealed to us that when the Hughes family are down in the dumps collectively, there is nothing they like better to cheer them up than a screening of these early TV shows. A real family favourite.

Jim drove us to these, and to gigs, in The Sound Affair's red Hiace van. Very practical. It could carry us all and our equipment: Jim and Sharon in the front, the children in the back taking turns on the wobbling deckchair. Preferable always to the hard ledge facing the keyboards and the elbow of a mic stand stabbing you in the face. (They can't give you points or revoke your licence years after the fact, can they?) Maybe it was the oncoming gig and nerves on his part but when we stopped, we stopped. Suddenly. When we moved off, we moved off. Suddenly. It was all sudden. There was nothing gradual. And the deckchair and its child became a very unstable bumping chair, often on the verge of beating them all to Dublin.

When he saw a red light he would speed up to meet it …

And he is Leo. It is me that is Taurus.

We did showcases for record companies and so keen were some eager beavers that they came all the way to Dundalk and watched us perform. We recovered from the let-downs by renaming those that had peacocked, all knowing and sparkly-eyed before us. And that would make us all better again. Just minor adjustments, really ...

And we were ready to brave another day.

Whelan's, a music venue in Dublin, comes into focus. Still largely papered, we were not quite the loudest whisper yet, but this was to bring us to America. A friend of John's, Bill Whelan (who would soon write *Riverdance*), had produced a few of our demos. He brought along Jean Kennedy Smith (the then American ambassador to Ireland), and having loved us, she invited us to Boston, to play the Kennedy Library for an American Ireland Funds event.

And it's our first time on a long-haul flight, crossing the Atlantic together. It's mind-blowing how innocent we are.

'They're going to feed us?' I disbelievingly asked John, and 'There's movies!!'

But the best of all, Sharon ...

We had been given the in-flight toilet bag, containing toothbrush, eye mask and the essential socks.

'Why socks?' asks Sharon, holding them out from her bag.

'Because when you hit a certain altitude, your feet swell,' John replies.

I did notice, in retrospect, she smelled the socks at this point.

Mid-flight, mid-movie, post-food, Sharon whispers to me,

'I don't think my feet smell … Do yours?'

And then the reason itself. Diplomats, politicians and networking eyebrows make up our audience. John had jokingly pointed to the exits when we were nervously sound-checking, in this glass-walled prism: 'If it's all going wrong, I will be leaving through this door.'

The speeches were endless and serious leg-stretching and bathroom breaks were needed by the time we began to play.

And it is, in fact, all going wrong. I'm singing to the exit when it gets even worse. A big, white-haired, grey-suited man is making his way towards the stage. He is on the stage and he is signalling for us to stop.

I close my eyes and in my head hear, *Could the owner of vehicle registration number … make their way to …* when he takes my microphone from my hand and, with gravitas, says:

'This band, The Corrs, they are our guests from Ireland and I want to hear them. So if you don't, please leave now.'

It was Teddy Kennedy, and needless to say we went down a storm.

From here we went to Los Angeles, knocking on record-company doors by day and sleeping on Judy's floor (an artist friend of John's) by night. Even the few that were curious couldn't really understand this Celtic pop sound, and so the doors … they closed like dominoes. We moved on to New York for more of the same, until a meeting with Jason Flom, at Atlantic Records. He was closer to interested and said offhandedly, almost as if he didn't know he was speaking out loud, 'I'd love David Foster to hear this.'

David was their in-house producer at the time, and in New York producing Michael Jackson's *History* album. John jumped on it but, though he tried, Jason could not get us a meeting.

Now it's a sweltering June day in New York. We are all dressed in black, carrying our instruments, when John realises we are close to The Hit Factory.

'Let's just go in,' he says. And somehow we manage to get through the sci-fi, superhuman bodyguards (perhaps through the V of their huge legs) and into reception.

'We are here to see David Foster,' John says with authority. David is called and appears down in the lobby. He brings us to a piano, where we play 'Forgiven, Not Forgotten' and a couple of others.

I remember he couldn't stop looking at the bodhrán.

'What is that?'

We could see he liked it, but many had before, and so our last night in America began.

The next morning John rang our rooms to tell us when to check out, car pick-up time, etc., and just before he hung up, he said:

'Oh, by the way, you're signed to Atlantic Records and David Foster is going to produce your first album.'

January 95
Suitcases on the floor
Scapulas and Violets
'Don't let them go's
Next door
Solemn lights in windows
Car leaving before dawn
The band that Jean and Gerry made
They fled the nest as one

Malibu, California

The sunshine paradise was drowning when we arrived. The cliffs crumbling into the Pacific. Towels at doors, and mud and muck up Sycamore Meadows Drive. The Irish had brought the rain, it seemed.

The studio was at the bottom of the garden, down a path, beyond the pool.

David's wife brought us fairy dust and wands, I think (or have I dramatised? … or had she heard 'Siog'?) and we knew we were on a different planet.

We got to work. The songs were there. It was just a matter of recording them, and I saw – and I don't use this word lightly – genius in David Foster. A generosity, too, as he happily had Jim co-produce, acknowledging the work that had gone into our demos.

Oh, I was wildly insecure. Painfully so. Grammys intimidatingly watching from every shelf –

'What's she doing here?' – and platinum records for wallpaper. He had just gotten three, I think, for *The Bodyguard*. Whitney Houston. And here I am the singer … need I say more?

I got bronchial asthma and lost my voice entirely and it became a bit of a nightmare. So many lead vocal-less tracks waiting. The songs unsung. Time. Money. I became so shy around David and asked to do my vocals with Jim, alone.

Imagine this? It is, without a doubt, David's forte. Just listen to every lead vocal on a David Foster production – beyond stunning. So, gift horse, mouth. Nose off, face.

That was me. Not for all of it, but for some. Ah well. It is forgiven, not forgotten, and it's history.

We were nearly finished and soon to leave, with our record complete, nearly five months later, when David walked into the living room. To Sharon and myself around Caroline on the piano, playing a song we'd just written. A song Caroline had begun at home in Dundalk.

'What is that?' he asked again.

And so began the time of firsts. First photo shoot. First video shoot. First actual CD in your hand. First ever time to hear our song on the radio. What David had come in on us playing.

And last shall be first: 'Runaway'.

Our name like a beer in the San Diego DJ's mouth. First promo tour. Voice wake-up. Five a.m. coffee. I smell hazelnut?

We sang and played to America driving to work and on the school run. Blankets over heads on red eyes. Another station. Another hour. Another city. Another day.

Bod Ron, Bow Ron, Coors, Cores.

Smile, photograph.

Autographs in case.

A family from Ireland.

You guys are great!

And you've got to hand it to America: no snobbery or 'too cool' here. It doesn't matter how, just get there.

So serenade in a back garden and hope she says yes.

On a turkey for Thanksgiving, laughing under big hats.

CD 1 stops.

Grip and grins.

In-store signings.

Play to win.

Play …

Because there's an aesthetic that blinds and dumbs. Though how, anyway, can you manufacture a family band, tell me? Test tubes?

But there is real beauty in this, because there's only ever one first.

And all is hope, promise and jet lag.

Our original bass player was Roland. On the surface he was perfect. Incredible time-keeping and precision, and he was so unassuming and subtle on stage. A real contrast to the spinning top at the mic. However, he became unreliable. Prone to fierce mood swings. He could pull a strop at any moment. We never knew when. Delusions of grandeur, maybe. I have a suspicion he was on the steroids. Ah ah … Dignity, Andrea! Anyway, he let us down one too many times, mid-song, mid-gig. Exposing us like Milli Vanilli, and we had to let him go.

Jim was reluctant, as he had introduced Roland, and was then – as he is now – a loyal friend.

So two tall young men, a guitarist and a bass player arrived at the factory one day where we were rehearsing for our first tour. Anto Drennan and Keith Duffy.

The pillars.

John had called them, forgetting (or did he?) to let us know that we were endeavouring to replace Roland with real live human beings.

Two, three, four …

Caroline counted us in to an entirely new experience that day. Liberating. As if we had been running in a walled-in and sterile gym before. Looking out of a small, square window. Keith has soul. So much feel and groove that Caroline was in heaven. And I remember forgetting cues to sing again, so blown away was I by Anto's playing. His guitar solos.

And it's likely they are laughing, reading this now. Because like the sky in Ireland, they are on the ground. So a perfect fit in every way, these adopted brothers.

But even they'd admit we were, and are, good together.

And we had a lot of fun.

The sandwich tour began and I had lost my voice again. Jim would often be sick before a gig, as would Caroline and myself. But that may not have been due to the nerves in our case. More likely a dose of hairspray poisoning, and that last look at ourselves in the mirror before we went on stage.

Mini, our monitor man, thought me a diva, I think. As no matter how loud I was (all the way to eleven) in my monitors, I still couldn't hear. It so happened, though, that I wouldn't need to sing. By the time we reached the west, the audience was singing every word of 'Runaway' back to us. It was all over the radio now. Spinning, as we bussed across Ireland.

And why 'sandwich'?

Because that's all we ate, except for a couple of late-night chip stops with Barry Gaster, who booked these early tours, until Keith threw a wobbly and there was ham and bread quivering for mercy on a Cavan hotel carpet.

He was a pioneer back then, Keith. Never taking his eye off the plight of the musician's rumbling stomach. He led the protest and the very first boycott on sandwiches.

We stayed at places like The Feeble Brown House in Sydney. The Rodent Inn by a motorway truck stop on the outskirts of Denver. The Holiday Bin somewhere with an

THE CORRS
IRISH TOUR ~ APRIL / MAY '96

APRIL	26	ENNIS, The West County
	27	CARLOW, Graiguecullen Hall
	28	CLONMEL, The Regal Theatre
	29	ATHLONE, Regional Technical College
	30	DAY OFF
MAY	01	LETTERKENNY, Mount Errigal
	02	SLIGO, Regional Technical College Hall
	03	CAVAN, Carraig Springs
	04	CASTLEBAR, Travellers Friend
	05	GALWAY, Leisureland
	06	DAY OFF
	07	DAY OFF
	08	WATERORD, The Forum
	09	BELFAST, Ulster Hall
	10	LIMERICK, Concert Hall
	11	DUBLIN, STADIUM
	12	BANTRY Mussel Fair,
	13	
	14	SHEPHERDS . IRISH EMPIRE
	15	

abandoned pool and tumbleweed. No holidays there for years. Towns and halls, where beds climb the walls, of bathrooms with ransom notes in sinks. 'Liberate toothbrush hostages from the clutches of "The Room Do'er"!'

Would you really want them back?

Yes. One could arrive into one's hotel room from the hotel bar, of a bleary weary evening. All excited for a bed cloud and the chocolate that just may be awaiting you there (defeats its luxuriating purpose, this chocolate on the pillow, I think. I will have to turn the light on, get up and brush my teeth again now. They don't show this in the Galaxy ads but it's a real mood-killer), only to find the room completely bare. No bedside lamps. No TV. No nothing. Just staring, surprised wall sockets and a blue flex, perhaps. There's the echo of the bed, chalked on the carpet. Proof that a bed had, in fact, been there. It's like a cordoned-off crime scene.

We travelled the world together and we grew in number. Like something that rolls and does gather moss. And we witnessed world wonders together. At least they were wonders to us Irish.

Black flies black out the windscreen on the road to Reno. Dangerous love. The love of the mating flies in a dark smoky cloud and the love of the driver. Who has driven now for thirty-six hours straight. Party bus, drive me to party plane, please.

And now it turns, faster and faster. It blurs with the speed and you can no longer see us, the spokes on the wheel. We are everywhere at once. I'd often have to turn back at passport control in an airport, to ask where we'd just come from. I had nightmares of doctor examinations with cameras on me, a spotlight in my eyes and a microphone to my mouth. Little did I know then that I had foreseen the future's reality TV. 'No' was not a word in John's vocabulary back then and so it wasn't part of ours either. And none of us would ever want to be the one to let the others down. So it was yes. To everything. We toured and promoted, all at the same time. Half-hour support slots, championed by John Giddings and Denis Desmond (whose desks our demos had providentially landed on), back to back with our own headline tours. In fairness to John Hughes, he was with us all the way, and not sipping cocktails with de blonde on a yacht somewhere.

He seemed to be moving always and to pace. This pacing intensified before our performances. I'd say there's a 'there went Johnny' path, worn side stage in venues throughout the world, in fact. And he seemed always to be thinking of ideas for us. Often completely wild ones, but the whole thing was wild so why not? Apparently the wildness was working. He made spider-web maps of possible scenarios and he talked of one wild day when we would sell our first million. And of another wild day when we would own one. Each.

He advised us to save our *per diems* in the winter of a radio tour of America. Minded them for us while we were people-carried through the crunch of a snowed-in and lamplit Pittsburg. And on through a snowed-in and deserted Buffalo. And on through a rainy and windy Philadelphia. To end in the brisk cold and optimistic breath of a New York morning, cash rich and spree happy, just days before we flew home for Christmas.

But what he loved more than any of this was our music. He loved what we made and how we played and sang together. It was *la raison d'être*, you see. It only stood to his reason that the world, once they saw and heard us, would feel the same way that he did. He just had to make sure that they saw and heard us. And so much was made of St Patrick's Day in New York. The night before playing the Beacon Theatre. Hours later, *Good Morning America*, live from Rockefeller Plaza.

So much he made of us.

His kids, John, Helen, Anna and Marie Junior, sat on the couch in their living room in Blackrock, Dublin, when we visited, their sunlit 'good' room where we signed those first contracts, like we were already and always the biggest band in the world. Shy and giggling they watched us like we were live interactive TV. (The remote is down the side of the couch, John …)

His own boy and three girls.

And de blonde has got to be honoured here. Marie was married but her husband travelled the world with another couple's kids while she mother-fathered their own through their school years. She lived the day in, day out in Dublin and, I imagine, looked forward very much to late-night,

117

early-morning, jet-lagged, can-you-hear-me? got-cut-off, phone calls from hotels somewhere in Exotica.

Behind every man, as they say.

There is no doubt: I would not have this story to write without the work and the love of de blonde, Marie Hughes.

Meanwhile, John could eat and eat and eat. The Reuben 'heart attack on rye' from Carnegie's Deli in New York – conveniently a few blocks from our record company. He discovered a restaurant that served layers of bright pink bacon and swimming pale cabbage on, of all places, Sunset Boulevard in LA. He ate marmalade with his eggs. He liked chocolate sauce with his ice cream …

He believed, you see. It was a vocation and it was a hungry one. And it could not put on weight.

He chose always to sit by me on aeroplanes to get my sausages. No chance beside Caroline. I would automatically pass mine onto his plate as soon as we were served. Though I did eat a green triangular seaweed thing beside him on the bullet train from Tokyo once, and he has never sat beside me as easily since. Just a little hesitation before sitting down and a sideways, not-so-sure look, assessing my mood and the drink in my hand. But that's probably also because when telling him 'I am happy, Johnny!' one day, I spilled my coffee all over him. We had just taken off in London, to fly to Australia.

He was different to us but we lived like family pretty much and we learned each other's ways. Him up at dawn in the kitchen in Malibu singing 'Runaway', the high bit, while Caroline and I lay on in the blue covered bunk beds of 'the crypt' (so called because its door was rarely open before midday) and Jim and Sharon likewise, in their own rooms. He also learned to turn a blind eye to family pool parties. Jean in the jacuzzi. Gerry playing the piano in his Speedos. Nothing to see here.

He understood an American LA weekend. All the slogs and sweats and dog-walking, coffee-holding, brunching, stretching, running upstairs to run down them again, juicing, unshaven, hanging-out cool of it. We would bring picnics to Zuma Beach or Point Dume, Braeburns and bagels, and eat pancakes in Paradise Cove.

Waitresses (actresses) loved him. His enthusiastic, direct air. So engaged in people. Buzzing, but with a kind of open shyness, too. A bit mad really. A different energy. A born Irish James Joyce Dubliner. The Corrs and Irish rugby. His Belvedere school tie. Philosophising on aeroplanes, St Thomas Aquinas, Khalil Gibran. Complaining when fellow passengers pulled down their window blinds and 'shut out God's good light'.

His spiritual friends and, by virtue of that, ours. Jim Moran SJ. And the ultimate gentleman, Ollie Campbell. Modest and brilliant and a man we are honoured to know. Ollie was our early patron.

Johnny and I shared a love of books and places of learning. Not long before we set off for America to begin this journey, we sat together on a bench in the gardens of Trinity College. On a beautiful bright Dublin day, we said

119

I would go as a mature student someday. Ancient is more likely now.

I put my school copy of *Julius Caesar* by his bed in Dundalk when he stayed.

He opened windows and fiddled with the air conditioning in the back of black town cars: 'It's hot back here.'

And if truth be told, he was never meant for the back-seat. For he needs to move and the room in which to do it. To be glasses-oning, jacket-offing, knee-rubbing, brief-case-searching …

He was a leg-stretching son of a draper man, yes he was …

He and I would go to movies on Second Street in Santa Monica. He liked popcorn with his butter. I didn't really like milk duds but I had them. It seems like every film we saw was special there, though. *The Madness of King George. Sling Blade. Brassed Off. Monster's Ball.*

He has been called the king of vague but it's the spider-web of 'what if's that cause the blur … I think …

His cup was always half full. Our clouds, when with him, silver-lined. He lifted our heads to the bright side (not always appreciated … 'No more bright side, please, Johnny,' Sharon said one day) and Plan BCDEFGHIJKLMNOPQRSTUVWXYZ … *ad infinitum.*

A few times I went alone with him to New York and into Atlantic Records and to lunches, dinners and meetings, as his 'little helper'. I even had a lanyard and laminate with my picture on it, smiling and wearing a

120

Christmas hat, beneath the words 'Johnny's little helper'. I don't remember who made that.

In the meantime, as we toured and promoted the world, comparisons between us girls came to be a daily treat. Always two-faced and hard on each of us, three individuals. If one is favoured, the compliment comes bearing the sting, the thorny rose piercing your palm, of another's weird and utterly unbidden rejection. It is all uncomfortable, in fact. And when you think about it, it is awfully rude, isn't it? Imagine standing beside your siblings as grown adults and a stranger telling you who is the most beautiful, who is the brains, who's the minx …

I have always thought my sisters prettier, but ultimately I am happy being me. And in any case it is how we see and shine out of ourselves that matters. And how we learn not to compare – ha.

Our faces age and change, but that never will.

Speaking of my face, I got a lot of rashes on my poor self-conscious face in those days. I could blush red out of the blue. No provocation needed. And then I'd blush about blushing because now it looks like I've had a bad thought and that my face is telling the truth and betraying me. Facecrime. That is how my anxiety and insecurity in the family free-for-all fish tank manifested itself, I think.

The rising red crept up my face like ivy on a flight to Venice once. We were to do a 'HUGE!' TV show there. Beside me, Sharon warily watched it grow and only when she was absolutely certain did she turn to me fully and say, 'Oh Andrea, I think you're getting a rash on your face again.'

I could get a rash about getting a rash, you see, too.

She had helped me the very first time it had happened, and has many times since. Trying to cover it up for me in the Ladies of the Berkeley Court Hotel in Dublin. Problem was, my face swelled too. Even bigger cheeks! Most of the time I just had to get on with it, do the TV show, blazing appendages and all. A literal scene-stealer. But this one time even the Italian record company recognised that in this state it would be best for our record and all concerned to hide me. We got a surprise day off in Venice, drank beers on a plaza and couldn't find our way home along the dark canals to our hotel. Sharon, the navigator in black, disappearing into black, re-emerging from the black ... Sorry, wrong way. This way. Not this way. Black in. Black out.

She was the navigator, too, in Amsterdam. Ahead of me again, but this time in a faux-fur leopard-print jacket. Bopping along the cobblestones, very busy Bet from *Coronation Street*.

Impossible to sneak into the hotel quietly, though, in this jungle camouflage and with the laugh of a hyena.

Anyway ... you get the picture. It was non-stop.

Eight hours of interviews. One small couch, four people. Everyone assumes, it seems to me, that families want to be close. Bodies touching at all times. Sure aren't we from the same womb. To a gig every night. At one point (a few years in, I might add) we rebelled, insisting

'A travel day is not a day off!' Arriving in Australia after twenty-two hours' flying, to realise we had a quick freshen up and interviews waiting. (Oops, forgot we lost a day!) Then another 'HUGE, cannot-be-missed opportunity' TV show, in France (honestly, our very lives depended on it!) emerges, so back to France from Australia. TV done and back on a plane to Japan, to complete promo and live combined tour. Then to Canada, on to America.

Four continents in three weeks.

We learned quickly to keep answers short. There are certain countries where they love highly detailed interviews. Every word in a lyric explained. All day, every day, for, as long as you now could remember, answering the same questions …

'What's it like being in a band with your family?' and Jim's all-time favourite, 'What's it like being the only boy in a band with your three beautiful sisters?' (Mmm – what??)

I could forget there was a camera on me, drift off and suck my thumb, only to be elbowed into the moment by whoever was closest. 'Is she all right?'

I remember our translator in Japan using many sentences to translate our now monosyllabic answers. She knew them off by heart. We weren't really necessary any more but at least we could snuggle.

And all the while there were endless ghostly hotel corridors. Dragging your wheelie bag through the fire-doors and down the steps, bump bump bump, and round

the sudden turns, keeping your bleary-from-the-tour-bus eyes peeled, while adjusting to this morgue's death light. And your wits about you, too, because 186 just may be on the second floor. Like hurdles on the obstacle course to your all-brown bedroom (after a night on the town there's nothing like a night in the brown ... your home from home ...) to find your key doesn't work (you're disqualified! Back to the beginning). Hotel elevators stood still on ground floors. Couldn't seem to muster the energy between us to press a floor number. Confusion over strangers that seemed to ghost us. Butlers in Kuala Lumpur. Bodyguards in Johannesburg. Notes from insomnia slipped under Tokyo hotel doors. Roppongi prince seeks likeminded walking dead for lobby-haunting and wall-climbing. Here's Johnny!

Oh if only we could've written the H word, then we wouldn't have to sell it door to door.

However. Now I've got the heebie-jeebies. I'll come back to that later.

But there were countries that adopted *Forgiven, Not Forgotten*, and us indeed, like we were their own. Spain, France and Australia. The latter interests me, now that I'm watching from the moon, and see a younger Gerry and Jean, strongly considering emigrating there. I am time travelling to a Christmas present. Two first-class tickets to tour with us in January. Cairns, Sydney, Melbourne. People queued up at an exploding in-store signing, to get their autographs.

Ouch now.

I am so grateful that we did that.

The UK, our next-door neighbour, eluded us though. Searching for our CD in the record stores only to find one (here it is!), cobwebbed and crying 'Mama' in the folk section. Obscure radio stations like hidden cavernous underworlds, which had you questioning whether you had indeed died in the 'Manager sole survivor' crash that John darkly joked about. But we were in the nowhere between Nirvana and Britney Spears.

And, it must be said, this was another time of terror. A time in which English buses were blown up by the Irish. Understandably, we were not so popular.

Oh, and then there was that radio gig when despair and resignation (the first and only time I'd ever heard John admit there was a chance we wouldn't make it till our second record) led to tears streaming down faces, please stop, painful, ab-inducing laughter.

Our record company had organised a radio showcase in London, enticing guests there with bottomless free drinks. It must be thirsty work being jaded, because it was a nightmare. Literally. Crazed angry drunks, like the cast of the 'Thriller' video, yelling through our set. We couldn't get off fast enough. We made it to our dressing rooms with 'never again's and 'that's it's, only for Sharon to arrive in last with 'Someone just puked on me!'

We had an inkling, then, that they didn't quite like us, but I was yet to be convinced. We were in the van ready to leave and I saw a skinhead woman and her boyfriend making their way towards us and I recognised them from the gig.

'Oh look … fans!' I said, rolling down the window and turning up the volume on their contorted faces.

It wasn't something a fan would say.

We skidded off to their Doc Martens kicking the van.

Time for the hardest record of all now. Number two. We go from nothing to lose, everything to win, to get it wrong and it's all over. Follow-up. Or down, as the case may be. It was so much pressure, as *Forgiven, Not Forgotten* had done enough to show our record company that we could be extremely lucrative. And people, and critics in particular, are forgiving (pardon the pun) on your first, but now the sound of knives being sharpened rang like a constant tinnitus in our communal Jean-pooled head.

Also, when can we write, while dizzy and spinning?

I am going to have to face the H word now, as this was the first time it was to rear its tiny big head. And once it did, I must add, it remained up there. It is here right now, in fact. Taunting and teasing: 'Nanananaaaa'. Like it is something you are so close to reaching, but never quite can. There were guitars and keyboards brought to hotel bedrooms and songs beginning, but apparently a 'hit' (there, I said it) wasn't something we could write alone. So the writing sessions in California began. Pairing each of us off with different, tried-and-

127

tested 'hitmakers'. Jim rebelled and continued in his bedroom.

I felt like I was made of veins in those days. With coffee for blood. It was unrelenting.

But there are songs that we all love now and that we would never have written alone. Relationships made and experiences had that we would never be without. Oliver Leiber, 'Only When I Sleep'. Glen Ballard, 'Queen of Hollywood'. Personally, I feel I became a lyricist then, albeit a quirky one. And there were days that the words came, like I was transcribing something that had always been. Like I was back on the bumping chair. Listening and writing into Mum's red lyric book again.

And at the end, home at last, where we never were any more, just as John had prophesied, only to hear it wasn't enough. It still wasn't there, but was back in LA, singing, 'You can't catch me!'

Finally we had it, a mix of self-penned songs and collaborations. So now to a listening session for Atlantic's über-important head of radio.

And the most holy of the insured ears are on …

The Queen of Hollywood.

She walked out.

And then there were full-on shouting matches between John and the company heads.

'THIS [fill in a raging expletive here] RECORD IS NOT COMING OUT!!!'

'"So Young" [a song Sharon had written in her hotel bedroom] IS NOT GOING ON THE RECORD THAT IS NOT COMING OUT!!!'

John knew we couldn't take it. We were, all of us, broken. We wouldn't survive it as a band.

He overruled. We flew to London. He walked into Warner on Baker Street and found us a champion. Andy Murray – not a tennis-playing champion, but a till-the-bitter-end, how-else-could-we-sweeten-this-life, music lover.

'Queen of Hollywood'

She drove a long way through the night
From an urban neighbourhood
She left her mother with a fight
For a dream misunderstood
And her friends they talk on corners
They could never comprehend
But there was always something different
In the way she held a stare
And the pictures that she painted
Were of glamour and of flair
And her boyfriend though he loved her
Knew he couldn't quite fulfil
He could never meet her there

She's never gonna be like the one before
She read it in her stars that there's something more
No matter what it takes, no matter how she breaks
She'll be the Queen of Hollywood

And the cynics they will wonder
What's the difference with this dream
And the dreams of countless others
All believing in TV
They see their handprints in a sidewalk
Flashing cameras on the scene
And a shining limousine

She's never gonna be like the one before
She read it in her stars that there's something more
No matter what it takes, no matter how she breaks
She'll be the Queen of Hollywood

She is believing in a dream
It's a loaded fantasy

Now her mother collects cutouts
And the pictures make her smile
But if she saw behind the curtain
It could only make her cry
She's got handprints on her body
Sad moonbeams in her eyes
Not so innocent a child ...

Now it is these non-hits, along with those that originated in Jim's bedroom rebellion – 'What Can I Do', 'I Never Loved You Anyway' – that went on to sell eight million records. Three in the UK alone.

Talk on Corners was everywhere. Singing out of car windows. The biggest-selling record in the UK by an Irish band, ever. It would seem there's an upside to not catching it, as people buy and love the whole record and not just a single.

The stars had aligned.

No, actually, there were particular hands lining them up. Simultaneously. Like hands on flint and into flame. Rob Dickins, along with a few faithful record company execs that didn't need to ask somebody else what they thought of it to know whether they, themselves, liked it. A Tin Tin Out remix of 'What Can I Do' and, most significantly, a cover of Fleetwood Mac's 'Dreams', remixed by Todd Terry, culminating in John once again capitalising on our Irishness and securing a live BBC broadcast of our St Patrick's night Royal Albert Hall show, where we were joined by Mick Fleetwood. Caroline and himself, thundering alongside each other through 'Toss the Feathers'. Happy twenty-fifth birthday, girl.

Overnight everything changed.

Forgiven, Not Forgotten was rescued from folk to tearful reunions with pop-rock friends, caught on infrared cameras in record stores throughout the UK. We became the first band since the Beatles to occupy the two top spots in the album charts. *Talk on Corners* number one, *Forgiven, Not Forgotten* number two. *Forgiven, Not Forgotten* was beside himself!!

'And I'd like to thank God and all my fans!'

And how to remain so grounded through it all?

Do a Spinal Tap in-store signing in Detroit, to two people (who I think just happened to be there) while this is all taking off, far, far away.

But there was champagne popping and dancing in a house in Dundalk, as they listened to the weekly chart countdown, each passing number, wondering, 'Where are they, Gerry?'

'All the way at the top, Jean!'

Can you imagine?

World tours, awards and platinum records followed. Helicoptered and motorbiked (not me, too scared) from TV shows to gigs, as every millisecond mattered. Six nights at Wembley, one at Earl's Court and a Scottish-accented reprimand from our tour manager, Henry McGroggan ...

'You need to learn to choose your nights, Andrea ...'

But there are no nights, Henry, and it would be deca-dent to sleep through this ...

Mum was now known to have one ear on the radio at all times. A single headphone in her left ear. One ear on her children far away while she typed and did her work in Dealgan Milk Products, a job she went about getting when she was forty-five. Endless A4s of 'Now is the time for all good men to come to the aid of the party' strewn on the kitchen table. And a glamorous teacher who looked just like Elkie Brooks on the cover of her album. Oh, 'Don't Cry Out Loud'. I love that song …

When we would call home from wherever, she would invariably tell us who had played us that day and what was said …

Larry Gogan played you today. You were the answer in Tony Fenton's pop quiz.

No matter how big we got, she did not change. Complacency somehow did not grow in her. It was always wonderful and worthy of a mention.

Even Gerry walking up the town to: 'The children are doing great, Gerry. What part of the globe are they in now?' That was ever worthy of a mention too.

Helicopters over Lansdowne Road. Forty-five thousand people making their way. Burger, hot-dog and merchandise stands.

And a breeze that makes waves of our faces
on T-shirts,
like flags leading them on
to pass the house with the steps
where our shadows pose still,
for those first black and whites ...

Side stage, John pacing, embracing and then releasing
To Lough Erin Shore
Side screens flicker on
And we are giants and dolls walking towards you
The curtain falls
The roar of love

Gerry and Jean in the mouth of the Roar.
Now I am bowed down with gratitude.
July 1999. She has four months left.

In April of that year, Mum had found herself 'breathless', would you believe, but it wasn't a good thing. From a benign (utterly friendly, if mistakenly, in retrospect) misdiagnosis of asthma, they were suddenly called back in to be told that she, in fact, had cryptogenic fibrosing alveolitis. Cryptogenic is probably the scariest word to me here, as it means this disease is not, as yet, understood. Though it has a different name today, it remains cryptogenic and it has the same sad outcome. We have now lost six of her nine siblings to this sorrowful mystery.

But suffice it to say that she breathed something, somewhere, at some point in her life that caused the alveoli to scar over. One doctor called it 'highly treatable' while another, more ominously, told her to 'get her affairs in order'. This left Daddy very angry.

How could you take away somebody's hope?

But I think he was just angry that we were losing her.

She was in the Beaumont Hospital getting tests while we were rehearsing nearby, to record our unplugged record. On a break, one day, I visited, but she was out of her room. An intern, seeing me there waiting, innocently let slip that a lung transplant was being considered. We hadn't realised it was this serious.

Mum saw it in my face when she returned to the room. 'She knows,' she said to Daddy, looking at me. And what she recognised in my face then, I see now, in us all, whenever this *Corrs Unplugged* plays.

It is beautiful, though. Probably more so because of this. And laughter and love did fill that Sheriff Street space, too. Mitchell Froom, this album's producer and a friend now that we have continued to love working with. His Hammond and his authenticity. Flying Quality Street and Fiachra Trench orchestrations. Fate again, as on suggesting we cover Phil Lynott's 'Old Town', we discovered Fiachra had worked on the original and written that joyous trumpet solo.

'Radio', a song Sharon had written the same day she wrote 'So Young', became the single, but it is R.E.M.'s 'Everybody Hurts' that is full of Mum.

Hold on …

She was no longer standing at the door waiting for me (in my mind's eye now, always wearing a yellow jumper over jeans), smiling the love out the door to me when I pulled up in my car. Nor was there the smell of roast chicken. She was on the couch. I should have known then. I ate at the table and talked in to her. This would never be Mum. How sick must she be? She was to fly to Newcastle with Daddy the next morning for tests and now had oxygen at home, which she used sporadically as if it was an indulgence. Like her lungs would get lazy if spoiled. I got her bag ready for the morning and meant to write a funny note to her to find within when there. Like the little additions to her shopping lists we made, too rude to mention here, that made her laugh in the aisles of the supermarket. But I didn't get around to it. I washed and I blow-dried her hair for her by the fire. I had never done this before. Oh, her head before me like our roles reversed. Her appreciation is too much for me right now. I noticed her fingernails. They come to mind a lot these days. The perfect white half-moons. The echo of their crescent in the oval tip. The ridges. But they and her lips were at this moment a little blue, I noticed, and we decided she should sleep with the oxygen tonight.

She is muted in these memories. As if I was then already watching through a veil.

In the airport terminal she walked to the Ladies while Daddy and I checked in for them. She took too long. I should have gone with her. Her eyes were so frightened when at last we saw her being pushed in a wheelchair by a young man. She had become faint in the Ladies and had almost fallen. A stranger helped her. I stayed and watched through the window long after the hospital plane had gone. I was rooted there. I felt I knew she would never return.

But thought was too painful at this time, I think, for the memories, they are not vivid. Not vivid enough now. Like the faded and faint little stars your eyes only discern when looking to the left of them. When looking beyond. They are barely shining.

The other day at home, I found a note she had made to herself. A note of prompts for what must have been her first doctor consultation. This line is heartbreaking:

137

'Can you make me better?'

She died in November while being assessed for that transplant, in Newcastle.

I had just gotten off the plane in Switzerland, where I was to write with Mutt Lange, when Caroline called to tell me I had to turn right back. That we had all been called in.

She was fifty-seven.

'How Could I ...'

I see you in the kitchen
Bare spuds in water
A red duck in a yellow pond
You knitted plain purl
I jump when I remember
Your snap and hand clap
Yourself you were
Your joy your joy
The loudest love of all
I see your hands on cards
Jack of spades
The queen of hearts
Cheeks flushed
Frightened eyes
Sore intimate
Sore truth
How could I forget you

Now it is really blurred, but it's not from the speed any more. It is my vision. And the worst part: seeing Daddy, alone. Imagining him in that house they'd built. The stairs and the stained-glass windowed doors that The Sound Affair bought.

Every tree they had planted and the seaweed for the soil from Blackrock Beach.

Now, the kind eyes of our engineer, Tim Martin, and John and Mitchell's shocked expressions seeing each of us, independently, appear in Windmill Lane to continue making our third studio album, *In Blue*. We needed to work.

Caroline's piano to 'One Night' and 'Hurt Before' had begun this. Both of which were the last songs of ours that Mum was to hear … in this realm anyway. Through headphones, lying in a hospital bed. This time I made it to Switzerland and stayed to write 'Breathless', 'Irresistible' and 'All the Love in the World', with Mutt Lange. He was so caring. I can't say much more.

A friend wrote me a letter at this time, I remember, telling me there would be blessings to come from this pain, this loss.

I believe they have never stopped coming.

'Breathless' went to number one in thirty-three countries simultaneously and is, to this day, the closest we have ever gotten to a hit in America, with *In Blue* achieving platinum status.

Dad travelled with us a lot from then on, but sometimes I think the hotel rooms, the luxury, the splendour, this rare and coveted world we now inhabited, made him worse. Seeing everything from bedspreads to curtains, to glasses, to cutlery through her eyes, and hearing and not hearing her exclaim, 'Look, Gerry!' appreciating every tiny, little thing. And what is a view when looking out at it alone, no one to share it with, and the absence and the empty seat beside you more present than anything else.

The deafening silence.

So he would often appear back in the lobby within minutes of entering his room.

'First Annual Report' by Gerry Corr

A year on my love
A year since we parted
You to the prayer wrapped unknown
Me to a cell called freedom

In your place I have memory
A stingy usurper
Dispensing crumbs
From the banquet of your table

Like a donkey in Omeath
Kicking my pride
And your laughter
Animating the Mournes

Or champagne Saturday
When we whooped and danced
To new celestial arrivals
On our cherished firmament

Your light is on dim now, my love
Yet blinding flashes of you
Startle me awake
From the barren limbo of my dreams

You'll be pleased God is back
He left when you died
Went a.w.o.l
Like he'd been found out
Not having the answers
And permitting instead a soothing indulgence
Why has Thou forsaken me

Yet there again, my dear
I must allow for pre-occupation
With glamorous new arrival
Introductions all round
Glasses raised and all that
Yours a spritzer, my love?

That's about it for now, my dear
Except to say the blubbering has ceased
And sorrow's sickly syrup of self
Expunged from the menu

Well ... in hope and prayer, that is
My love

Reeling in the Years has just come on the TV. It always makes me cry and today is no different. The year is 1970. The anti-apartheid march and the controversial housing of travelling people.

This is precarious 'Here we go' ground that I am on now, so I will tread carefully. God knows, the world does not need another preaching pop star. And I am reminded of the essay for the Leaving Cert exam that I did not choose: man's inhumanity to man. Probably because I was as uncomfortable with the subject then as I am now.

But what is the point of this human life if we, who are fortunate, do not endeavour to help those who suffer?

Did you see the Muhammad Ali documentary, *When We Were Kings*? Did you see how he spoke in what was, to

144

me, an everyday voice, with everyday language, on racism. Did you not respond 'Of course', like I did? It wasn't shaming or guilt-inducing. It was enlightening and inspiring. He was inciting love. And if someone has the power to incite the opposite, as is happening today, surely someone good could come along and flip that hate to love. And the rabble, the mob and the herd instinct in us all would redirect towards unity, tolerance and equality? Simplistic, I know, but couldn't this be utopia if we all could just ... get along?

No, it's more selfish than that.

'Love thy neighbour as thyself.'

And there are so many wrongs that are simply wrong, glaringly so. It doesn't take a creative eye to see that.

The first time we would use our celebrity in a significant way was when the Omagh bombing occurred, in which twenty-nine people were killed, a woman pregnant with twins among the dead, along with three generations of one family. Innocent people (we see it every day now) who didn't realise they were leaving for the front line when they left their homes that Saturday in August.

We were at the height of our fame and all five of us, John included, sickened. Indeed the whole country was, and beyond. We organised a TV special in Ireland for the victims, and U2 and Bob Geldof, among others, joined us.

A father in the audience that was made up of those, the left behind, will stay etched in my memory always. His face. His mouth a broken line. But more than anything, his grace.

145

When an artist – Bob, I think – (sincerely) expounded and raged at the horror of it all, spewing vengeance, this bereaved father said something like, 'It is that, that has us here in the first place.'

And our years reel in to one of our greatest blessings. The 'someone good'. The leader to incite love. Forgiveness. Dignity, Grace. Nelson Mandela. Madiba. I see my family as beyond fortunate to have met this man and to have played for him five times. When he received his honorary doctorate in Galway, we played and everyone was seated and reserved, until he himself stood up to his full six feet and danced to 'The Joy of Life'. Now that is a vision I do not want to lose. Caroline's first child, Jake, as a baby, got to meet him when we played at his eightieth birthday. We played Africa Day in Trafalgar Square, and the 46664 concerts in Cape Town and Hyde Park to combat poverty and HIV/AIDS in Africa. I sang 'Is This the World We Created' with Brian May. What a privilege that was. He had only ever performed it with this beautiful song's co-writer, Freddie Mercury, before this. But most special of all was being among the few artists, Annie Lennox, Peter Gabriel, Brian May, to fly to his safari residence in Africa and sit around Madiba, under the stars, as he told us stories.

And the idea, the truth most impactful of all to me, is that this charming and elegant man with such humour in his eyes had suffered so profoundly by the hand of his fellow human. We visited his cell in Robben Island, where he spent many of his twenty-seven years as prisoner 46664. It is barely long and wide enough to have contained him lying down. It is almost coffin-like in its narrowness. A kind of death in life. To have risen from this with such a love of, and a faith in, humankind is awe-inspiring. And now the Charlottesville horror, and one of the most retweeted quotes in the history of Twitter:

'People must learn to hate, and if they can learn to hate, they can be taught to love, for love comes more naturally to the human heart than its opposite.'

We received honorary MBEs from the Queen, the monarch next door, for our charitable work and contributions. The first complete band to receive them since the Beatles, and the first ever Irish band. I imagine the Royal Family was fully aware that we are from Dundalk. 'El Paso', as a journalist so cleverly (albeit only to himself) christened it.

And to a few, it may have seemed controversial. But we chose to ignore that, and its suggested hypocrisy.

Talk on Corners, as I said, was all over Britain. The peace process was underway. We were seen and recognised as Irish, but also as brothers, as the same. We gratefully accepted all the love, awards and applause we received as we toured the UK, and similarly, we now accepted this honour.

Dad is photographed with us on this day. Playing with Jim's head, trying to make him laugh. And, though she is missing, he is smiling here. That is a good memory.

And the reason I felt prompted into all of this by 1970, was that Daddy was part of that anti-apartheid march back then, and also fought for the travelling people. A journalist called him 'the weirdy beardy'.

Now that is funny.

'Harmony'
More walls since Good Friday he said
There's nothing good about that
Down Bombay Street
There's flames at our feet
And they burn like the Indian sun
It's a far cry from home you land
Your brothers and sisters behind
This battle scar's long
Like a mourning song
You know though you never had learned

Now we'll never know the man you'd have been
The one who brought peace to a land born in pain
Taught love to a daughter
Kindness to a son
But you've ended before you've begun

And a main street became the front line
My beloved a casualty of time
It's wrong, it's wrong
No matter what side you're on
To end them before they've begun ...

Thinking of Nelson Mandela and that particular quote on love, I am reminded of a non-fiction book that I read that had an impact on me: *The Human Animal*.

And it told of love and how it causes our pupils to dilate when we feel it, or get a rush of it. Or, the most wonderful, that as a baby, your pupils are dilated all of the time. So that someone, when looking, will think the baby loves and needs them and so they will pick the baby up. Our little pupils communicating so much. The idea (eyedea ... sounds like a real part) is so sophisticated and beautiful that I feel it could only be God. The droplet that falls from the sky into the water and radiates to wash-paint the briefest, most beautiful sun. 'So good of you to drop in, welcome!' It can be every day ecstatic to be a witness to that moment.

Cause and helpless effect. Automatic. A reflex.

Love is our greatest reflex. It is what our eyes want to do. They want to be crying-laughing, heart-eye emojis. Like the glorious stretch they will live on in the pinpricked lonely darkness. It is true for all of us, I think.

I believe in our goodness. And while our heads are turned daily towards the darkness and towards hate, I

149

choose to focus on love. I feel like rebelling when I watch the news these days. It seems to me a particularly shameful time. But no, I will not accept that we are as pathetic as depicted and resign myself to our doom. A race to be pitied if not just to cringe, crawl and blush about. Let's begin a rebellion of love.

I believe we could get better and that art, throughout the ages, has been trying to show us this. I see redemption at the end of a book. At the end of a life. The final paragraphs in *A Tale of Two Cities* are to me the most beautiful and inspiring. And these particular lines came upon me in a sort of eureka moment:

> *'I see ... the vengeance, the juryman, the judge, long ranks of the new oppressors who have risen on the destruction of the old, perishing by this retributive instrument, before it shall cease out of its present use. I see a beautiful city and a brilliant people, rising from this abyss and in their struggles to be truly free, in their triumphs and defeats, through long years to come, I see the evil of this time and of the previous time of which this is the natural birth, gradually making expiation for itself and wearing out.'*

And that made me really happy. To be reminded once more that there is no new sin and that we are on our way, though it is indeed 'gradual'. And to think that no matter how we modernise, when we fight and kill each other, why we fight and kill each other remains the same. I have registered and tipped my Border Town girl hat at the complications, but there is a centre and it is peace. Where the pendulum rests is love. It does not waver or doubt. It is not judged and it does not judge. Love is where we begin, where we proceed to end and where we never end.

I hope.

I think we are decadent. And I mean from that, not that we indulge too much (if drinking tea is a worrying sign, then I think we can gather that I have no problem with overindulgence), but that we waste so much. We waste so much happiness and beauty while we fight over it. Like your children fighting over a toy: 'It's mine!' and you take it away with a 'Nobody's getting it now.'

And you bomb it.

On the news today I watched an illegal immigrant scale a building like he was Spider-Man. To save a dangling four-year-old boy. A stranger who is legal but a refugee nonetheless. The spirit in his little body fleeing a civil war. Seeking asylum from neglect.

The eyes dilate in love, like they are drinking up all the light.

The story of humanity could be a love story.

Rooms

The rooms we frequented. This one ornate and solemn. The Vatican.

His Popemobile made him appear as if to float by our pew. Don't catch Jim's eye, whatever you do. Daddy with us, and I am brought back to a day a long time ago when I let go of his hand, and he lost me in a field in Drogheda. The east coast leaned into the water of the Irish Sea with the weight of a third of Ireland's population. As if the island itself had fallen to its knees in reverence. I am surrounded by walking skirts, trousers, shoes and boots, on mud-worn, trampled grass. My five-year-old self carried away from my family on a skyless adventure that smelled of wet coat.

So I did not get to see His Holiness on this occasion, but twenty years on we would sing the 'Oh Holy Night' we had sung yearly to Dad's family, for Pope Saint John Paul II.

And the maestro enters a white-walled rehearsal room in Bologna. White towel draped around the shoulders of a Hawaiian shirt (could this be right?). Imposing, jet-black sooted hair and a baton taps one, two, three to …

Silence.

I imagine, now, the hush that followed orphaned Oliver's 'more' and all eyes are on us, including his …

'Mm … Please excuse us, maestro, but we do not as yet know the song …'

And here is where the aesthetic is at last appreciated, by us. For his entourage breathed a sigh of relief with not just a little nervous laughter. Which led us to believe that in ordinary circumstances, this would not be tolerated. And thank God we learn quickly, in Italian too, because he waited for us and then we went out, he in a dress suit now. And all the Italian children sang '*Oi Vita Mia*' with us.

Glorious. Pavarotti. The stage floor beneath our feet seemed to tremble in homage, when he sang.

And now 'the family from Ireland' sing 'Oh Holy Night', again, (and the ghosts of the settee chuckle far off … 'I told you it was good!') … but this room is in Clinton's White House. Bill's towering and learned focus is like an etching in my mind.

'God Only Knows' with Brian Wilson on a stage in the garden of Buckingham Palace. Thankfully I was all laughed out at Jim's 'bumbubumbubumbu-bummmmmmmmm' backing vocal by the time you saw us.

And Paul McCartney watching while we sang 'The Long and Winding Road' so slowly, each line drawn out and drawled, like we really meant it. Like we needed you to really understand how terribly 'long' this winding road was.

Caroline could not hear any of us in her monitors (that's a lonely place to be, believe me) and as we all know, too fast is worse than too slow, so she committed wholeheartedly to the latter. We set off at dawn and reached our destination, your door, at twilight the following week.

Having toured the world again with *In Blue*, we returned home to record our *Live in Dublin* record and DVD. Mitchell produced and played with us again and we persuaded Bono and Ronnie Wood to join us for a couple of songs, friendships having been formed when uniting for Omagh and also having played support to U2 and the Rolling Stones in America. Blessings and musical high times for us all. 'When the Stars Go Blue' and 'Summer Wine', 'Ruby Tuesday' and 'Little Wing', orchestrated and live in front of an audience again. So the tension never leaves and we are suspended for always here. I think this transcends and it's what you feel when you listen and watch. Luck and just a 'little bit of magic'.

All beauty all fade away
All moonlight return to day
All sunrise all shooting stars
All earthbound bare feet in clay
You know we're standing on
Borrowed heaven
All heartache all rivers cried

Don't stay out too late tonight
I love you, don't wanna die
You taste like paradise
I know I'm breathing in
Borrowed heaven
You gave me life and
I will give it back
But before I do
I'm gonna hold it tight
This is my prayer
All body all skin all bone
All silky all smooth and warm
All pleasure all pain are one
Almighty I stand alone
I know I'm living in
Borrowed heaven

Borrowed Heaven follows *In Blue*.

It is digital pop, as if we are trying to squeeze sunshine to warm ourselves again. This was to be our last studio record of original songs for a decade, but we didn't know that then. Olle Romo, whom we had met when working with Mutt, produced this, which we recorded in Dublin, in LA and indeed Africa, where we sang with Ladysmith Black Mambazo on the title track.

A vivid memory that I have of this time is, strangely enough, of another band. 'Summer Sunshine' was our first single and throughout the week of release, we were battling for the top spot. I woke in my bedroom in London with the windows open and the most beautiful song serenading from an open car window. It billows the curtains, into my bedroom, into my ears … And I know there's no way we have beaten this … Keane's 'Everybody's Changing'.

Defeat can sound sweet.

And everybody was changing, in our world. It was my opening line in 'Summer Sunshine':

'Everyone's changing, I stay the same'.

Sharon had married, as had Caroline, and now Caroline was pregnant with her second child, while touring this record. She moved from the drum kit to the bodhrán, out

front, when the baby grew too close to the snare. I remember one day in particular in our dressing room in a venue in Liverpool. I heard her on the phone to her husband Frank. 'Did he just talk?' she said, almost frightened. Jake, her baby, hadn't said his first words, but she got very upset before the gig and I knew and understood that this time with her was running out. She would have to choose for the moment and Georgina, within, was also pulling on her. They needed her and she needed them. Ultimately she left us to tour America without her and returned home to her own young family. Keith's brother, Jason, joined us as drummer. I see now how amazing she was to have stayed so long, and also how hard it must have been to watch the carnival move on.

The children, by the way, are a testament to that pivotal decision.

And the corners soften and melt,
to become arcs,
and the arcs join hands,
and it's time to go home.
Around the lyric book,
still smelling of the smoky pub fug,
and the metal of the music stand it sat on,
her hands on the pen,
on the pages,
Dad's, a Chinese lettering,
the chords above her words.

The yellowed paper,
dog-eared and listening,
holding on still,
to the applause.

We gathered with Mitchell, Anto and Keith in a studio in Dublin to make what is, to this day, one of our favourite records. One that we have all admitted to playing in our time apart: *Home.*

We embodied our past and that of our parents and learned the songs that they had played before us, embracing exclusively our traditional history. The Celtic without the pop-rock. 'My Lagan Love', 'Black Is the Colour'. And a song that I will always find hard to sing without crying, 'Heart Like a Wheel'. Indeed, Jim and myself recorded it live, in one take, for this very reason. They were all then orchestrated by Fiachra, again. And if you listen really carefully, you may just hear Caroline's second child, Georgina, making her cooing, gurgling baby sounds, in harmony with her mum, her uncle and her aunties.

There were strangers dangerously close to infiltrating. Romantic visions of … what?

Domesticity??

Dissension in the ranks

Blinkers thrown off one by one

Peep sneaking at imagined personal lives

That didn't include

159

Suitcases

Deadlines

'We talk'

Small couches

Hairdryers like breath

The colour brown

Democracy

Headline angst

En masse

Pigeon-holes

And a definitive lack of a clean white page.

On one of our final tour dates, we made our last live CD and DVD, *Live in Geneva*. Caroline rejoined us, now a mother of two.

John knew he had a chance against men, but cried off, defenceless, against the little people.

The small but deadly. The babies! So as we raised our hands for our final bow, that snowy night in Ischgl, he bowed his head side stage and raised the white flag.

N ow the stage goes dark.

The personalities hang empty, inanimate, though close still, in flight cases. Shoes assemble with the dust of untold stories of stages throughout the world. The ghostly Braille of their tired soles. Echoes of glory and 'Do you know who I am?'s rustling in silk. Hierarchies forming in the blackout.

'She wore me accepting that Brit Award, I'll have you know!'

'Well, you could have done a better job of protecting her modesty!'

Guitars, keyboards, violins, bodhráns, drums, whistles, huddled next to each other in lock-ups, and the question moving between them:

'When oh when will this get boring?'

And back in the house three doors close …

Keys turn and lock.

Jim, Sharon and Caroline. Retreat into their private, longed-for worlds.

A Solo Cello Outside a Corr-us

Although I wasn't where they were in their lives, I was ready to hop off and move alone. There were the stirrings of independence and individuality in me. As, of course, there were in us all. I had unrealised dreams. More ordinary and everyday visions, but dreams nonetheless. Behind the smile where anxiety hid from John's 'never home's and Daddy's 'rule the world's. Behind the blushes, there were things that I was never brave enough to say. To admit.

My Leaving Cert results were good. I remember a bright afternoon in our living room, all of us there, and Mammy being torn. Torn for me. She suggested tentatively that I could do both, third-degree education and be in the band. But she was quickly dismissed. Caroline and I had only applied to a few universities in the unlikely case our heads fell off and we could not be in the band. And they had waited for me, the baby, to finish school. While waiting, Sharon worked in a music store and came home with the summer of the Cocteau Twins and Rosie Vela. She and Jim also formed a trad duo where they played locally in the same rooms that Mum and Dad so often had. Sang and played songs from their book. Songs we would later seek out together.

It was just a fleeting moment of a question that didn't even seem to suspend for a millisecond in the air between us. For it fell as soon as it rose. A blind fork in the road where fate took barely a second to decide. I looked at her wondering too. Hoping, maybe, in that single moment, that this scenario may be possible. But we all turned left together. Then.

Now, in retrospect, I know how lucky I am that I did not have to decide my entire future at eighteen. It all happened. A unique education. And just how lucky I have been in my life so far, I cannot quantify in words, though I am trying. Back then, though, I didn't know that.

So here was my chance for individual choice.

If my head had indeed fallen off, I would have liked to study English Literature and Theatre. Stories made up of words sung into music, they had always formed pictures in my head. Five-minute dramas, in which I was the character. When eventually we wrote, this was still the case, with characters sometimes imagined, and sometimes true. Sometimes deemed fictitious, to hold on to the truth.

To play a part. To act. I felt offered the chance to experience without the personal fallout. And when someone else has written the story, then I am not accountable. Be 'it', or indeed 'she', good or bad.

Wow. Maybe baby isn't brave at all.

But it feels instinctive to me to want to feel what it's like to be somebody else. Try you on. To fall down the well of your story. Something I have always done in my head. From the bumping chair to right now wherein I am predominantly Mary Duane on *The Star of the Sea*. I cannot in truth tell you why.

Sharon Rabbitte, a deep-thinking girl of few words, was the first film character that I was to inhabit. Though on the surface, involving only three lines, each of which was the same, one might imagine that this would be a breeze. However, as Roddy Doyle had largely written *The Commitments* in the lesser-known language of Swearish (spoken throughout Dublin and parts of rural Ireland), it required some method acting. I was not very popular so, around this time. But we suffer for our art and I think it paid off. Don't you?

Actually the overdub that we recorded was in fact more offensive and made us laugh a lot.

'Go and shite!' became 'Go and vomit!'

I stayed in Jury's Hotel in Dublin. I can smell the soap now. See the flower on the paper wrapping. So many hotels that I have stayed in since, but this was the first. In the evenings I was too shy to be around strangers in the lobby. Felt I'd stick out like the impostor I was. So I'd walk out to a shop in Ballsbridge, close to where I have a house now, and buy chocolate, Cadbury's Golden Crisp I remember. And that would be my dinner for one, looking out on the Dublin night through the window of my room. And the Dublin mornings on the set on Synge Street smelled of burnt coffee and seemed perpetually waking but never fully awake. Ever in the half-light. And I am there with Johnny in these mornings – 'John', then. Hair slicked back and protecting me now. Protecting me as this one-time stranger always would, for some strange reason. The clever lunacy.

Jim had to chaperone, too. I wanted to be grown-up cool and in the pub like the Commitmentettes. I didn't appreciate his fraternal guard, even though he always brought me out with him and always included me, a teenager without altitude. I had nothing to complain about. But I did complain. Judas'ed him in a way, in my diva-shy, on-the-cusp confusion. He told me that I was not nice any more, one morning, and it stilled me. The possibility that what he said was the truth. The folly and fumble of my try-it-on youth.

Mum was my chaperone for the overdub recording. Our first ever visit to London. Me then just semi-sweet sixteen and she forty-eight. We stayed together in the Hilton on Park Lane. Golden-chandeliered, head-rising awesome to the two of us then. A bit of 'What's she doing here?' too.

We queued up for the Hard Rock Cafe, I remember, in this surreal London night. Like we had entered the Tardis, she and I. Had fallen from the couch watching *Doctor Who*, and had ended up here.

We didn't get in to the Hard Rock, as it happened.

Pigeon-holed even then. Too pop.

And the mistress cried in Alan Parker's *Evita*, not only because she was yanked out of her lover's bed and her post-coital slumber. But because her chance to express how she really felt, her song, was stolen!

Oh well, I understand. It is a beautiful song.

And then there was Anne, in *The Boys and Girl From County Clare*, who, when not falling in love, rowing with her poor mother, Maisie, or playing the fiddle without moving her fingers, loved nothing better than a few late-night sandwiches (washed down with a glasheen or three) in Ballygally, Antrim. Three witches, one broom and a ghost. She was a bit of a drinker if the truth be told, and thus appeared a tad bloated of a morning.

And Car Hen all to myself, too. Another vital presence in our story is Caroline Henry. The red coat *Hi-de-Hi!* witch with an unfortunate talent for organising. Tall,

167

ghostly Cork girl ('never put your shovel where there's no gravel', 'two tits in a bun', 'her auntie Biddy Shmiddy and pain is it?') who will make you laugh till you cry and make you feel so lucky you are with her and that you are alive. The appreciation is like my mother's. Lots of 'look!'s said, and then you see. The turf fire. The trees. The glasheen in your hand. The intricate, tiny-handed artwork on your cup. Rick Stein's food descriptions. Car Hen makes you see and feel so lucky. How wonderful is that? These are the only friends we need to have. Illuminators. But there's endless 'homework', too (signing a million album covers – why didn't I just sign 'A' to begin with? … 'Baby C, did you do your homework?'), but again I just feel so lucky. Because she just laughs and she loves.

Finally, Lily (poor Lily) of *Broken Thread* who was, sadly, dead … though at large in the Himalayas. This movie never saw the light of day, which leads me to question my choices. Maybe this wasn't one for the method acting.

I, also, had written songs on my piano in Dublin.

Little picture songs and stories. I loved Björk's *Debut* record and Nellee Hooper's production. So visual and evocative. And it was avant-garde, for me, in that the tools he uses to paint with are more often technological, and not live instruments. Apart from the orchestrations, it is without a doubt quite a departure from The Corrs records. But having said that, I could never have created a Corrs record by myself. There are four of us. Four writers. Different combinations. And no matter where the song has originated, be it one of us on our own, or two or three of us, it becomes what it is through the attention we, all four, give it. Thus we share the credit.

Bono and Gavin Friday introduced me to Nellee and I played the songs on the piano in his studio in London. With Nellee standing behind me, unknowingly reminiscent of the terrifying piano lessons, I managed to get him to commit to producing my first solo record, *Ten Feet High*.

And I learned to be scared of the H word in all of its forms. Because 'That's a smash hit' can ironically be more worrying than 'Where's the hit?' I learned that one is indeed the loneliest number, and that the 'we' we had needed a break from was something to miss.

I had been uncomfortable in interviews before, but at least I could be quiet and hide behind my hair, when there were four of us. Now I have full responsibility and

169

accountability in good times and in bad. No one to share either with, I found anti-climactic and deflating.

But I love, and am proud of, this record, as is Nellee, and if I were to do it over again, I would make it exactly as it is. Ten years on.

'Ideal World'

Jeanie marries when she's twenty-one
She has a baby one year on
And every year that's the way that life goes
Lost herself in domesticity
A feeding, cleaning entity
She can't recall what she was before
In an ideal world kids would keep their rooms tidy
An ideal world he'll be home from his work on time
And in the morning I could lie in ...

Johnny signs his share of autographs
For all the people he makes laugh
And he walks home to an empty flat
Does his best to fight the silence
Late-night TV, Vicodin
He can't forget what he had before
In an ideal world she would still think I'm funny
An ideal world she'd be waiting in bed for me
And in the morning we could lie in ...

Molly's sitting in a waiting room
The top doctor will see her soon
In the body nature gave her
Worried if she'll ever wake up
Wondering if she's better off
Why can't she be what she was before
In an ideal world he would still think I'm pretty
An ideal world he would only want bed with me
And in the mornings we could lie in
In an ideal world you would make a decision
An ideal world you'd be making a home for me
And in the mornings we could lie in
Sunday mornings we could lie in ...
In an ideal world

There were days and nights in this time I am looking back on that seem now blessed in a magic light. Living in my doll's house, Birdie's nest, the rabbit hutch. A yellow-bricked, sash-windowed mews on Heytesbury Lane. The lane that Caroline and Frankie also lived on. The twisters bookended. Her room down a gravel hall. Dragging closed the wooden gates in the evenings or the afternoons either and shutting out the world. Dancing on a reinforced wooden table that never gave out, no matter how many feet trod on it. My own blue NEFF oven. Dinner and wine make my brown eyes benign. The skylight above my bed. Waking one morning, basking in the glow I was bathed in like a newborn's

171

first wonderful glimpse and the phone ringing beside my bed.

'Bosom! Have you seen the sun?!'

'Yes, Bosom! I was just wallowing in it. It's beautiful!'

'Not the sky, Bosom! The paper!'

In the light of that late summer, early autumn, I felt like I was suspended in the heightened awareness that it really is all borrowed. Suspended like a leaf. A borrowed heaven. Gavin Friday and Bono on either side of me walking in Merrion Square in Dublin, feeling like it was the perfect place to be and we three the luckiest alive. Walking where our ancestors walked. When I felt that even the leaves on the trees knew that they were in their final and most beautiful moment before they would fall. They glimmered amber and gold like the colour of my girl's hair.

Bono and Gavin, along with Maurice Seezer, had written a breathtaking song, 'Time Enough for Tears', for the Jim Sheridan movie *In America*. We walked from the light into the gloaming of the Davenport Hotel and drank champagne before we emerged giddy into the glare of the day. We played while we worked; our work is our play, you see. I sang the song in Maurice's house and later my brother Jim would ask Bono and Gavin how they brought that vocal from me. 'Time Enough for Tears' was nominated for a Golden Globe and, wearing as gothic a Christian Dior dress as I could find, my Nancy to Gavin's Sid, I went with Gavin and Jim Sheridan. The Irish in LA. During the award before the 'Best Original Song – Motion

Picture' category, I looked around nervously, noting the expressions on both the winners' and the losers' faces: remarkably similar. As if the losers were as delighted that they had lost as the winners were that they had won. 'Hell, yeah! [Clap clap clap clap] I am a winner losing to that winner!' Gavin, however, did not seem to notice this good-sport protocol, or if he did, he did not believe in it. The camera's red eyes blink into life, the robots circle our table and the spotlights blind. 'And the award for best original song goes to …' It was not us. I began to clap. And Gavin in the glare of the spotlight said, 'That's a fuckin' shite song. We're being overrun by fuckin' hobbits!'

From here I am led to another family, the Mundys.

When my agent told me that the Old Vic theatre in London was casting for *Dancing at Lughnasa*, I scrubbed off my gothic eyes, threw on a housecoat, and showed up to read for the part of Chrissie … pretty much. I believe Brian Friel to have been one of Ireland's, indeed the world's, great playwrights. And it is at this moment that the theatre hooked me. Coming from the world of pop music, it was liberating in its complete lack of vanity. No playback. No post-mortem. Very little glory. Just the knowledge that you all, a few hundred people, felt something in a room, went through something together, one evening, and then it was gone, disappeared off into the ether. As an art form, it is, to me, a real expression and celebration of our humanity. And you would want to love it, because it is hard work. Eight shows a week, one day off, until you emerge three months later.

I created a few mondegreens here, too, in my complete lack of experience. On opening night it is traditional for the actors to give each other cards, I was told, to which I whispered to my closest Mundy sister, 'What is the significance of carrots?'

And I thought our director was telling us to 'march' with the kite, at the end of the play, when she talked of the proscenium arch.

Interesting idea.

Before we opened, we had a dress rehearsal for Brian Friel. After which he came up to me, kissed my cheek, and said in his Donegal lilt:

'You're lovely.'

Now there is more glory than I could ever need.

In the meantime, a not-so-strange stranger, a friend of Jim's, had infiltrated my world. On realising through conversation that we had been in each other's company many times, I asked him had he not liked me before. He replied that he had thought me beautiful, but that he had also thought that I was 'in the corner writing poetry about death'.

Looks can be deceiving ... or can they? So Brett and I married, the August after I had finished the play.

And it seems to me now that he saw the truth of me then, which I had yet to meet. Maybe this is what human love really is. Recognising who their other is, before they truly know who they are themselves.

I pretend for a living. He couldn't pretend if his life

depended on it. And the Picasso face of his truth is my beautiful face. And there is no deficit in the leg.

For I meditate these days in a graveyard, when he is at work and the kids are at school.

Hush. I think I may be a witch.

Breathe into the yew tree and ask to hear the voices and absorb the stories that are told in tears now. Tears newly shed for all their silenced early pain. The dew on my evergreen branches.

Voices my neighbour, the crow, describes as 'stilled'.

Let me sway in your air till your tears fall down my face. Use my living hand, my beating heart and my undying hope for this world of mortals to unstill your voice, so through your death you can teach us how to live.

And now more characters to play, though this time through song.

After I sang on a charity record, 'The Ballad of Ronnie Drew', in Dublin, John Reynolds, its producer, approached me with the idea of making a record of covers. Songs that I had loved and had not written. I was reluctant at first, having had quite enough of solo records for the time being. And I had found myself more predisposed to the word 'no' in this time. Once you say it enough, it's actually quite a nice word. Paradoxically positive. He soon persuaded me, though. And the luxury of just being a singer and interpreter of other people's work appealed to me more and more.

John is a special man. As his parents were special people before him. They fostered twelve children and John lived as a foster child among these children. Such generous, loving spirits they were that they mother-fathered them all the same. And so inherent must this love and generosity be that John saw it as a blessing to have to share their love. Remarkably and so refreshingly non-judgemental, this English Irishman. You are good as you are. You are actually the better for the gritty bits.

We made a record of songs that had marked moments in my life, engraved, like the lines reaching across my hand. Songs from the bumping chair. Lifelines. This was a joy. A choir made up of a thousand Brian Enos in Donna Summers, state of independence. Billie Holidays, I'll be seeing you, saving me (and, I must admit, the guests) from making a speech at our wedding. A small tour, a big laugh. Falling up the down escalator in a German airport and laughing at the word *Ausfahrt*. Caroline joined us for 'Breathless' when we played the Union Chapel in London, and Daddy was there, too.

I did an interview around this time in which I was randomly asked whether there had been a teacher in my school years who had had an impact on me, growing up. There were a few, in honesty (Mrs Crilly's 'clean as you go' still in my ears when I cook, Mrs O'Hare and my essay on our garden – 'Shadows stretch, long and skinny …' God, I was at it already), as I liked school and think I was lucky

177

in my friends and in my teachers. But I mentioned one in this interview, from my primary school.

I was about seven, I think, and to my shock, they had chosen me to play the princess in our school production of Hans Christian Andersen's *The Princess and the Swineherd*. In an early rehearsal, I ran off the stage, crying, and into the cookery kitchen next door. I couldn't understand why they'd picked me and was so overwhelmed and shy. My teacher calmed me down, sat up on the shelf of the window in the kitchen, and told me that she knew that I could do it.

And so this leads me to the opening night of *Jane Eyre* in the Gate Theatre in Dublin and receiving a card (not a carrot) with a simple message written in it:

You can do it, Andrea

Love Mrs O'Donaghue

I cried taking my final bow as Jane and withdrew to my room.

We have reached the intermission now. The curtain is down. What will we play while the whispers grow to talk to laugh? While knees creak their yawn to a satisfied stretch … ?

Harry Nilsson singing 'Everybody's Talkin'', I think.

Banking off of the northeast wind
Sailing on summer breeze
Skipping over the ocean like a stone ...

Skipping over a ten-year ocean
The orchestra Gerry wanted
The band he got.
Skip a generation
To a chamber octet ...
And the greatest blessings of all ...
Jake, Georgina, Ryanne, Cal, Flori, Brandon, Jeanie and
    Brett.

The Mama Eye

I, now, am a hand-squeezer with a traffic-conducting head.

Non-optional extras include blinkers, tiger blood and hi-fi, bomb the bass sound.

Always read the label before crossing.

Side effects may include vomiting, diarrhoea, feeling funny, a loss of libido with or without stomach pain, a funny feeling and death.

Adverse side effects may include having to cross Edith Grove yet and sorry for your trouble the lamp-post flowers.

And in and out and in …

Hahhhhhhhh with a deep inhalation before finalllll ignitionnnnnnn

haaaaaaaaaaaaaae

'VRRRRrrrrrrrrrrrrmmmMMMMMMMMMM. Come on, babas!'

I cross Beaufort Street
on the King's Road.

'No Go Baby'

Walk on by my fruitless market
Hills and hips and heartache
Tear stain kiss my swollen belly
Angel echo there
But it's fading
I am wasteful

I still feel you
No go baby
I still want you
No go babe

Spring clean your room
When I'm asleep
Light, housecoats and vacuums
Put me back
All spick and span
Brand new
Like you weren't there
Yes I'm brand new
New born virgin

I still feel you
No go baby
I still want you
No go babe
I'm so sorry

No go baby
I won't hold you
No go babe
I wrote this song a long time ago
Before you ever were
About another little soul
Who never made it here ...

I have miscarried five times. The first and second the most devastating, as I could not see yet what … who, I would later be blessed with. I walked and I prayed. And my mother-in-law, Pat (a blessing in herself), prayed and lit a candle for us every day. Torches and tallow lamps, often to 'the little flower', St Therese, for whom there is a shrine in the church of St Jean.

'To the right and to the left, I throw the good grain that God places in my hands. And then I let things take their course. I busy myself with it no more. Sometimes, it's just as though I had thrown nothing; at other times, it does some good. But God tells me:

"Give, give always, without being concerned with the results."'

It was Easter time the first time, and the most lovely and inspiring man, a Jesuit priest called Father Brennan, who has just recently departed, said something to me that will never leave me. When he congratulated me on a pregnancy that was sadly, unbeknown to him, no more, I cried and he said:

'After the crucifixion comes the resurrection.'

Father Brennan taught my husband and many of our friends.

This he would write on the blackboard every morning …

'Life is a mystery to be lived, not a problem to be solved

Faith is not against reason, it is beyond it.

If you don't stand for something, you will fall for anything.

Good judgement comes from experience, experience comes from bad judgement.'

My friend prayed for us in a special church in Laghet and Pat and myself later followed. (We will forget the bit where she nearly killed us, driving on the wrong side of the road, after leaving the church later … ehhh, Pat!! Something to paint and pray for, straight away …)

When you enter this church, you see its walls adorned with everyday people depictions. Drawings and paintings of who and what they are praying about. Accidents, illness, forgiveness, mercy. All the more affecting as they are more often than not painted with an inexpert hand. All the desperate love, hoping for a cure and to keep who they love with them. Or even to let them go. It is so beautiful and sad.

But really there must be something. A room with all that desperate love and hope in it.

That is where and what God is, maybe. The room of love and hope.

And the moment I stopped reaching for those I could not hold was the moment that I saw all that I have.

Brett, Jean and Brett.

After the crucifixion comes the resurrection.

So how could I continue this story without speaking of the greatest blessings? In whose dimpled, impossibly soft hands sit the world's wonder and its redemption.

Their era that you who reads, and me who writes, will be one of which we are no longer a part. Ghosts looking out of picture frames. Old stories and visions of a past in which people terrorised and killed each other. But we loved each other, too.

And I am praying that this love could be the majestical light that defeated the dark history they read about. Just another Grimm fairytale.

We are advised to live in the moment. I believe we do have to look beyond ourselves, though. And that which is beyond us, is before us. They and their children will be there. There …

And will there be polar bears, elephants, tigers, whales, tuna, salmon, Syria, Korea, Africa, Israel, the USA, the un-United States of America … this is endless … But there is an end, actually … Will there be oxygen?

Will there … be?

Jeanie has just turned six and yesterday I talked to a teacher regarding a concern I have about a friend hurting her feelings and it hurts me, as I am sure this does most parents, to think of her open spirit and innate happiness corrupted. That she will think of herself as smaller and feel ashamed in any way. Because I certainly remember the labour that brought on the birth of my self-conscious-ness and it is a sad and new beginning … The history behind it, a dreamy unreality.

Blissful ignorance.

A terrible beauty is born.

The teacher welled up, though it's an ordinary everyday playground tale, and advised me to nurture other friend-ships because 'this world needs beautiful, naturally kind people like Jeanie.' (Oh Jeanie, you'd better be kind if you're reading this … Is that a burden? It could never be a burden to be kind, could it, love?) And this made me think … I am not telling this to say my daughter is extra-ordinary, though of course she is, but …

187

This is where it starts, and if that is true then it also could be true that this is where it stops.

'Galileo' is what I listened to while I danced in the kitchen with her in me. My heart could ecstatically burst to the opera of Jean.

A Happy New Beginning

Brett and I moved to Washington DC and lived in Georgetown on Prospect Street. By *The Exorcist* steps (perfect), and Georgetown University. And I had dreams of attending and studying literature because when you think of it, my head now had fallen off and better late than never. But through the surreal days of an earthquake and Hurricane Irene, I discovered I was pregnant. Oh, I love that life. The electricity inside. The most beautiful secret. Lying in my bed just me and a baby that I didn't know was girl or boy, but that I knew I loved. Every bite you take imagining your secret, yum-yumming inside.

Her birth was dramatic and traumatic for both of us, though she, thankfully, remained strong throughout. The wee trooper.

I did not. I nearly died. Blood transfusions and worrying heart irregularities that brought in more doctors and machines. But God is she worth it.

Worth dying for.

If I'd been in a developing country I'd likely no longer be … And she …?

She wore a pink faux-fur coat
Over OshKosh dungarees
And she drove the streets of Georgetown
In a pink convert a bling
Pushed by her mother
Just a stranger mum that sings
'Skinny marinky dinky do'
Like she's flying without wings …

'I love how you love it,' my inner delight says to her, watching her ride a bike for the first time. Her face is like a light beneath a watermelon helmet and strawberry-blonde curls. She actually shines. An almighty, a creator, if there is one, could only look upon us with these mother-father eyes, surely? And if we made God up, then why did we make one up that is ever scolding and judgemental?

'Love it, but don't love it too much.'

Even I don't believe in him.

The world is a wonderland. I don't think we could ever love it too much. When you think about it, it is all going wrong because we are not loving it. Not loving each other. Not loving ourselves.

I laughed my way into labour with our son sun, Brett. We went to the cinema and watched *Anchorman 2* and

I doubled over holding my basketball belly, and laughed every second step of the snowy walk home. He was born in a blizzard and I certainly could not describe the experience as a laugh, but it was a breeze in comparison to Jeanie. I received a bottle of Burgundy from a mysterious friend named Ron when we brought our baby boy home and he, 'Booboy', is to this day laughing and smiling. As if that really was where it all began for him.

I wonder. Maybe Mammy laughed herself into labour with me. Washing the floor is the only story I remember. No, maybe not … That's never funny …

The happy, smiling boy is so very funny! He has no pants on now. Just a red-and-navy striped T-shirt and he is in downward dog.

'Mumma … I'm going to do yoga!'

Ha … and now he's teaching Jeanie, who happens to be appropriately dressed, wearing a shiny blue leotard.

'You need to do this, Jeanie …'

My headphones on him and he is listening to 'Man in the Mirror' and shouting, 'Mummmaaa … Michael Jackson has the hiccups!'

And Jeanie says, ever practical, 'He should have cancelled.'

Oh, 'ever practical' reminds me of Sharon. Now we can't call this blasphemy, can we? She was only a child. Just as God made her …

Jim came home from school horrified about the awful story he had just heard. The story of a man called Jesus Christ …

'Who was nailed to the cross!'

And this has me bumping again …

'Sure he'd fall off if he wasn't nailed, Jim,' she said.

I just told them that the 'will-o'-the-wisp' is their souls that will go on forever. Jeanie was getting all yuck about the bones and the blood.

One day we were at the soft, hard opening of an extravagant hotel in which there was entertainment for our children laid on. While we, the adults, the grown down, up down ups, celebrated, babysitters watched as our children enjoyed first a magician … who was brilliant! Appearing doves and all, and I nearly wanted the kids to move aside so I could watch … But then there was a pirate whose gags seemed to be predominantly about how badly teachers are paid, and I noticed Booboy sitting on the babysitter's knee. I walked him out and around the hotel and we happened to pass the magician, having a breather (… feeding the doves … no, he wasn't really). Booboy let go of my hand, ran back to the man and said something that made him roar laughing. I had to follow and ask, 'What did he just say to you?'

Through his laughter he told me that 'He asked me to make the pirate disappear …'

Oh, I hope you are ever smiling, Booboy. My sun son.

He calls the candle by me a prayer candle. And he keeps blowing it out on me.

'Now the prayers are going up to heaven, Mumma.'

I think they are, too, Boo.

'It becomes all children, especially girls, to be silent in the presence of their elders,' I read in Charlotte Brontë's *Shirley* today. 'Why have we tongues, then?' the daughter asks …

I have said that it was remarkable to me that my father's mother, Alice, was so religious, but now I feel that it would be truly remarkable if she had not been. If she had not sought comfort and strength in an Almighty. For surely she needed her faith in a Divine and in eternal bliss more than I myself need. When she died, a neighbour consoled Dad by saying that Alice had 'never sullied her baptismal vows'. 'Sullied,' I say to myself. Why the reference to dirt? Oh, I think, it's just not compassionate at all. Yet I, too, feel the need to have faith. And again I excuse this subtle shaming by reminding myself that it's just the dress that man puts on God. Or the surplice. Humans are writing the rules and to be human is to be fallible.

There is a truth that I have sidestepped on this walk. In deference to my daddy and indeed my husband, who are both good men, good husbands, good fathers. The truth of the disparity and inequality that still exists between men and women. My mother's assumed role was to run the house and to shoulder the greater portion of the work regarding us children. A mother's work was never done, yet Daddy had his weekends off. She was working in Hallidays, the old Clarks shoe factory, when she met Dad. This work was naturally dispensed with as soon as they married, a given at that time in Ireland. An unwritten law. Or was it actually written? What if she didn't want to give this up? What if she liked it? These questions have been neither asked nor answered because I suppose what could be the point? But can you imagine the books we have not read, the music we do not hear, that could have been composed by these muted talents? The cures found? The theories constructed? There has to have been more than the few dim lights we have seen escape kitchen windows. I think of Irish writers and I list, as you could, Joyce, Beckett, Wilde, Yeats, Shaw, Friel, etc., and I realise I have to google to find a woman. Of course I find some; Google is good. But they are not in my head or on my tongue and the few female names that are, are known because they inspired great men. The woman. The muse. The literal helpmeet. Could we possibly be so different to each other? Two souls fated to journey in the body of either a man or a woman. Could it be possible that only one soul has the capability to play an active part in cultural history and that this is dependent on its gender being male?

Virginia Woolf said that in order to write, a woman must have 'money and a room of her own'. I have the annual income, I earned it, but I walk to write, seek two hours of solace and then I return to my motherly duties. Sporadically I pick up my phone to type the thoughts that still swim and in these moments I can be asked what I am doing. I feel a little sneaky almost. This guilty pleasure. To write is a guilty pleasure. Imagine. I have a hangover from my parents' male–female interaction as my husband has a hangover from his. It's difficult sometimes to decipher whose hangover I am suffering under. I am sure my husband believes it's my own. I suspect he is right. I remember when Mum got her secretarial job in Dealgan Milk Products, having not 'worked' in years. Quite an achievement to get this position when you think of the young, single, educated competition. I was in the hall, having walked in from school, and was poised to tell her that I'd been caught smoking when she turned round from the kitchen window and told me that she had gotten this job. Caught up in the relief that this good news might afford me, I disregarded the tentative look that she had when she told me. Like she was guilty. Guilty of wanting a little of her own thing. Guilty that we all were not enough for her. Tentative in case we might object. I regard this moment in my mind's eye now because I recognise it. The kitchen window is replaced by a mirror and it is me that I see. I have a strong impression, though I do not remember it being uttered, that she worked even harder to maintain our home so that she could never be denied the freedom of her work. *If everything continues as smoothly as before, then I will be allowed to do this.* I feel

194

the same in regard to my writing or drawing or thinking, even. Once our home runs well I can do this. I do not imagine that men think these thoughts.

It's interesting, anyway, and it makes me think of the hangover we might give our children.

Things don't always run smoothly here. Sadly not, for it is oft a jagged and perilous terrain. Because of this guilty pleasure I nearly flooded our apartment. Boo had gone to the toilet and he needed Mumma and then Mumma thought this might warrant a bath so she turned the taps on and returned to this pleasure. Some time later I asked Jeanie what she had spilled on the kitchen floor. I turned up to a kids' party three weeks early last weekend. And speaking of parties, I just cannot master sending a Paperless Post kids' party invitation. The first year the invitees were bewildered to read that they were being thanked by two strangers for the beautiful flowers they had never sent. The second year I invited Jeanie's wee friends to what we in Ireland call a push-through. The party was to begin at 11 a.m. on Saturday and finish at 1 p.m. Sunday. I could go on …

Act 2

A ringing phone. Fumble in your pockets. Thank God it's not you. Oh, it's not anyone's …

Curtain up.

It's on a box of Pampers, on the stage …

'Hello?'

'Hi, Andrea. It's me, Caroline!'

'How did you get this number?!'

Beeeeeeeeeeeeeeeeeeeeeeeeeeeeeeeep.

Only joking (ah, Gerard). But the second act does begin with a phone call from Caroline. Blame the drummer. She didn't want to regret not trying to do anything together again. Be it a tour, an album, she didn't know, but what's the harm in seeing?

So the four got together again, in a rehearsal room, organised by the fifth. Beneath a train line, in Putney, in London. And maybe it was the train that did it. There's a line across from our house in Dundalk. You can see it when you play the piano in the purple-walled room, or when you sit on the window sill and sing around Jim. But we knew pretty quickly that we were not finished.

Each of us played and sang, nervously I might add, what we had done, individually, on our ten-year 'break'. But it was Jim's piano to 'Ellis Island' and 'Strange Romance' that was to begin *White Light*.

And it was happening. We had unknowingly boarded the train and were moving along invisible tracks, from red to amber to green.

And I never really admitted to myself that we were doing it again. There's an anxiety that comes with the joy of motherhood that had 'I can only do my best' repeating like a mantra in my head. And I had a lot of irrational fear, as I imagine we all had. That we would be swept away into the mirrored hall of our past, where we ate, breathed and drank this life. And that my children and my new life would somehow no longer be. (I did say irrational.)

Whenever the idea of resuming our work had come up before, either from John or our record company, I had always felt very negative about it. We had chosen to jump. We were not pushed, and so we went out on a high, and it is that image that endures. We are immortal there somehow. Spared the indignity of a desperate descent.

But the music that was coming from all of us, the songs, I found worth that risk now. And that's my subconscious I am recalling. As I said, I was not admitting it.

For all these reasons we made most of this record off the radar, without letting our record company know we were doing it until we absolutely had to. I think that is why the writing and the making of *White Light* is closest to a first record. We allowed no outside pressure in, for as long as possible. We worked away ourselves, meeting Chris Young in Chestnut Studio in London every two weeks. Writing and recording simultaneously.

As my children are the youngest, my siblings made it easy for me in that they travelled to London. So I would walk to the studio in the morning and walk home, for six o'clock, and resume mama activities. And I think it felt tenuous and precious, for us all. As if one of us might drop out at any time and it would collapse, so shhhhhh, tread carefully.

We had learned real respect for each other and an appreciation, in our time apart. And now we knew what we hadn't known before. That we did not have to do this. That we do not think the same, because we are a family. And that the magic in the four of us might actually be our contrary opinions running riot, and not our genetic closeness. Until, at last, they settle. So it is not easy. But anything worth doing could not be without some discomfort.

I have heard it said that you can only ever be as happy as your least happy child. And maybe it is no accident, then, that this was the time our dad felt he could go. He had hoped, in our closed-door years, that we would reunite and that he would be side stage once more, watching us. Preferring it there beside us, to out front. He felt more a part of it there. He does deserve this final applause.

Jim, Sharon, Caroline and Andrea were together again. Doing what he considered each of us did best. No lost skittle, lonely and vulnerable to the wind. But bolstered again with John. His work was done. And he had been so brave to continue for so long without his love. Missing the way she said the word 'milk' and his name 'Gerry'.

On the Monday of a studio week, walking into work, I talked to him on the phone for what was to be the last time. He was in good form. Had had a good night, as he would say. He didn't sleep well any more. He was looking forward to meeting Gayle, the sister we had made through Jim, and his grandson Brandon later that day.

I remember that day having quite an existential conversation with Jim, about moments of awareness of Mum that we both had felt we'd had. And sometimes I think now that I felt something brewing. Crying watching Sia's 'Chandelier' video and Sergei Polunin dance to Hozier's 'Take Me to Church' …

When I tucked my children into bed that evening, Caroline rang to tell me that Daddy had had a heart attack.

And this is the story of a blessed passing. So many 'could have's avoided. Like, he could have been on his own and not meeting Gayle and his grandson, that day he walked into his beloved town for the last time. I met an old man once who groaned as he painfully and slowly lowered his exhausted self to sit on a park bench beside me. He said, 'Old age is nothing but a series of indignities.' It was not that for Daddy. He walked three miles every day. His mind was sharp – well, as blurry-sharp as mine is. And he had faith. His daily prayer was 'In God's way may we be united again.'

He pretty much resided down memory lane with Mum at this point, and I imagine, at eighty-two, on one of his sleepless nights, he must have wondered how and when he would go. Did he turn back and take one last look at their home after he locked the door that day?

He had outlived many of his friends, his siblings, his son and his wife. Moving on to join them doesn't sound so bad.

They used to sit by the fire on a Friday night with a couple of gin and tonics, and Mum would say to Dad, 'It's good here, isn't it?'

Well that is my prayer. That she is saying exactly that, to him and to Gerard, now.

We all had three days around his hospital bed. Swallowing the tears back into our eyes, whenever he opened his. And making him mime-laugh, the only way he could, all rigged up. He had been christened Patrick Gerard, and so the nurse, whenever she would ask him to try and not move his leg, would call him Patrick. I told her if he did it again to say, 'Gerry, put that leg back down, lively!' as that's what he used to say to us. 'Get up those stairs, lively, and do your homework, lively,' or 'Put your bike in the shed, lively!' … 'Tidy your room, lively!' …

The matron – coincidentally from Dundalk, as was the surgeon – said to me, at a moment when I was out of view crying, looking in at him in his room, 'This is good.' God knows, she knew how lucky we were, getting to say good-bye. At one of these moments he nodded from the bed as if beckoning one of us back in. So I went in and he mouthed 'Thank you' and I said, 'Thank you.'

And that was it.

'Stay'
Prayers float as coloured letters to the gods
Make mine a land without compassion
A melting pot of pain
Stirred slowly to the boil
We had a radar now it's gone
This is a cruel cruel love

I'm stood on the dark side of love
This a cruel cruel love
I'm stood on the dark side alone
Let love light your way
And forever always with me stay
I'll live while I'm alive
But forever always with me stay
Still reeling though I knew you'd one day go
There's no softening this shock
Write me a song and throw me back upon your knee
Help me move forward
Now I've lost where I began ...

It is dawning on me that this is, in fact, a barefoot pilgrimage that I am on. And the ground now, the cruel and jagged rock beneath my feet, where the red stains the blue, makes me want to be lifted like the crying child I was on Communion Day. The mirage is of velvet pebble, at least, if not moss that tickles. And I'd say my sisters and brother feel the same way. But it is tears and grief that made *White Light*. The waves would come on each of us at different moments. As if we were passing the baton in a relay. We are all at the surface now, exposed and raw. Moments of hilarity ... the dark humour we'd inherited ... to crying again ... With no real difference between the laugh and the cry. It's like we were all mad, absolutely untethered, and aloft. Holding on to each other through our music.

I had whispered in Dad's ear when he was no longer opening his eyes, when he was dying, that he could go. That we would be OK. And I sang Sarah McLachlan's 'Angel', his favourite song, about Mum, in his mind. Because there is no way you would get to do this, to die, a better way, another time. And it comforts me now when I recall that he was completely without fear. He knew, and he was ready. This gives me faith.

Parents teach you how to live and to love and I imagine, to die. They do it all first, before you. Like a mother tasting a little to check the temperature, before feeding her baby. And through all that they had survived, the devastating loss of Gerard, their parents, friends, neighbours ... and then for Daddy, the loss of Mum, they taught us to survive. To live and love on.

Until we meet again ...

So you see now that this is the band you had before you in Hyde Park, five months later. September 2015. Our first gig in ten years. This is why we cried when you sang 'Runaway' … Why John cried and his daughters cried, side stage. And I'm back to loving strangers, because that is who you are. Thank you.

Tears of St Lawrence
The night sky
I cried for you
For the ones that we've lost
That we're missing
Bid adieu
Celestial goodbye
Lay now and rest
And I'll do my best
To start again
I begin again
Why do we always notice
What's been taken
And shout to the world
Everyone
My faith is shaking
One moment's change
I'm drinking to trust
And surrender
And come what may
And begin again …

The welcome you gave us at that Radio 2 gig not only overwhelmed us, but I think I saw it in the eyes of our record company when we got off stage: there were more than embers in this grate. It may be possible to fully reignite. But with the bellows came the outside pressure. Some of which I am grateful for and some I am not. Songs appeared in our Dropboxes. The 'hits'. Here we go again.

We had produced and written, to my mind, our best songs to date. What we needed was a producer to take some of the burden and direct us to the finish line. I did not believe we needed songs. I think, also, that I was more precious than ever about what we did, now that both our parents were gone. The broken-hearted place that these songs had come from. And we were not making this record to be number one. If that were to happen it would be incidental. So the baby and the eldest swapped positions and I was heading for a bedroom rebellion of my own.

'Why are we talking about other people's songs?' I would ask …

'Do you think Brian Eno and Daniel Lanois, on hearing U2's *The Joshua Tree*, said, "Hey, Bono, wait till you hear what I wrote"?'

And I can hear you say now, 'You are not U2 and this is not *The Joshua Tree*.' But what is the point if you, yourself, do not believe in the integrity and the quality of what you are doing?

Anyway, I didn't follow through and I am glad that we co-wrote 'Kiss of Life'.

We were highly vulnerable to being undermined, John included, and finished this record in a cauldron, John Shanks joining us in London for the final three weeks. Then Jim on the phone to LA, trying to get the mixes right, through the night, so that we would make our November deadline.

You might imagine this record, so, to be melancholic. But it has the other reaction to loss, fighting through the darkness. Defiance. Life. Now they are gone, we are closer … we are the top layer. Facing our own mortality, we ask what and who will we be, before we go. Honour thy father and thy mother. Honour the gifts that you have been given, in sharing them. Gratitude.

And it's a release from that room.

The mantra now is 'Look thy last on all things lovely, every hour, every minute, sweet' … The whisper in the rush. From first single to photo shoot, TV show, performance … Sharon and myself, dancing side stage, watching our sister, Caroline, go on first, and her silhouette come alive on the curtain. This may be the last, ever. And whoever heard of getting a second chance twice? Truisms, paradoxes and deep joy. A record fundamentally about death and life that is not morbid. Telling yourself not to let your fear sabotage your – perhaps – final performance, and at the same time, forgiving yourself, quickly, if it did a little bit. As it isn't life or death. You know that now.

Joie de vivre.
The joy of life.
Carpe diem.
Quotidie.

And don't call it a tour, whatever you do, or I might not manage it. Let's say a few gigs. But it was a tour and it was exhilarating and I don't believe we have ever been better together. We toured *White Light* through the blackest rumble of terrorism. But there was something about that that intensified the energy, the love and the gratitude. The Bataclan, where we had played a sweltering and memorable gig so many summers before, ever present in our minds. But it only made me love you more. The night we played L'Orient, Bastille Day, we finished only to hear the Nice attack had happened and sat up in our hotel lobby watching French TV, horrified by the scenes.

We arrive in Brussels on a Sunday and it is like a ghost town. Looking out the car window and I am scared, because I am not with my children. Asking myself do I have a bad feeling, and giving myself one in the asking. Armed vehicles and soldiers on empty streets. Our hotel like the one in Stanley Kubrick's *The Shining.* I lie in my room, close my eyes and listen to my audiobook, because that is what calms me … and when the lift doors open, later on when I'm leaving for the gig, I audibly gasp, because there are three armed soldiers waiting to enter it. One of them smiles at me because he saw.

God, I feel sorry for us all. I am a coiled spring. But three hours later, I stretch out on stage and I am willing to go with you. And our songs take on the meaning of the time. 'Bring on the Night', 'White Light', 'Stay'.

And then Kew Gardens. The most beautiful summer evening, just days after the Nice attack. The world on high alert. Aeroplanes overhead. Thousands of people brave the beauty in the time of terror. And our front row … a girl in a hijab, a beloved lesbian couple, black and white, all creeds, all colours … There is no division. There is no intolerance …

There is only love.

'Three Robins'
Changed
I am changed
Forever altered
Losing you

Three robins will rest
On the step of the sill
Looking in at the girl they grew
Chill myself out
Too much one night
Felt the glow of the afterworld
Talked to you
Cried my Pandy heart out
Every word that I said was true
Thank you
Thank you
Thank you
What we said in the end
Was true ...

The story of how the robin got his red breast is beautiful to me. I read it to the children last night. If we could return compassion and poetry such as this to religion ... Oh how would our world be? The thorns in His crown. The little bird soul tries to remove them and in doing so the red blood of Christ stains his breast.

When Daddy had just died and we were in that timeless fog, sitting in our living room, his coffin in front of the organ, talking to the priest about the arrangements and the eulogy, I moved my eyes from the priest to a robin resting on the window sill behind, and then another robin joined, and then another ... And the three looked right in at the crying girls and boy they grew. This is true.

It's a seismic shift when you realise you have no parents left … At least it felt like that for me. And the pain avoided the first time around comes to meet the new rawness and give the current salt and a brutal force that threatens to drown you at times. To realise nobody will look at you like that again. I used to catch Mum across a room watching me. It was all love. No one will love me like that again. And now Daddy. I had come to fear this from the moment she died and now here it was. The goodbye that I had begged them not to say was, at last, said. Golden silhouettes in the doorway …

We asked him the questions we did not get to ask her. Advice on babies' sleep, food, etc., and we no longer now had even his speculative answers, or 'Your mother did all that. I'm sorry, I don't remember.' Bold Gerry, a man of his time … never pushed a buggy, changed a nappy, made a purée … I think he felt foolish then and a bit embarrassed to admit he had obeyed the domestic laws of the Irish time (for they could short-change a man) and that he regretted the lost chance to be a part of these everyday acts of love.

He pushed our babies, thank God, rocked and held them and made them giggle, pop-popping his lips together, blowing on their tummies. Things he must have done to us. I used to leap from the kitchen countertop into his waiting arms.

He loved hugs himself. Was starved of them. When I linked his arm we both felt what he missed.

210

My boy Brett and Daddy have the same forehead (five-head, as my husband calls it).

How Mum would have loved that time. I'd say nearly more than any time. Her drinking in of the present, and of her children's celestial ascent and glory, was in part because she blindly believed, like we all do, that she would reach these, the most blessed of times, too, and live them with us. She wouldn't have needed an earphone to hear us then. She would have been around. She would have helped us. She would have loved our children. Her grandchildren. So much.

I think it was bittersweet for him to watch us love our babies as he had watched her love us. He would remark, 'That's so like your mother, Pandy,' and it was in those moments that I would become aware of her absence seated still by his side. The one he was never unaware of. The one that never left him. That he never got used to.

He never stopped missing her.

I will never stop missing them.

Curling orange peel on the stone bench behind me. The sea sparkling the setting-sun light, into this tree cave where I've rested the summer long. An offering, perhaps, from a previous pilgrim. The holiday is drawing to a close, as this day is to an end. Years and miles beneath my feet and the blue paint chipped in abeyance of my superstition. For I move from pagan to Christian in a Lughnasa dance. Magpies saluted, Hail Marys, Glory Bes, but most of all, Lord:

Make me an instrument of Thy peace,
And let me just hear them
Tell the story
In the breeze
And let me just write it
Here.

The flame ignites, blinds white, to the smoky fog of the Peruvian wood and the hands of a guru.

I am back at the beginning.

* * *

The satellite to *Jupiter Calling* was first spotted in the breakfast room of a Berlin hotel. John tells us that maybe it's time to start writing again and working on the follow-up to *White Light*. (Wouldn't that be heaven, Johnny? Well, it's in the sky at least.)

We were just releasing our second single, and were thrown. But the world we had rejoined was changed. Pop-up emails in the windows of our sunglasses and a perpetual west-scrolling river of attention deficit beneath our eyes. We are back to one week on, one week off, write, record, a song a day, prejudice and early dismissals strictly forbidden. In a small studio with a grand piano, in Notting Hill. On our weeks off we were virtual-writing. Melodies, songs, lyrics, chord progressions, Garage Band, into the microphones on our phones. Press record, 'Quick, quick, get it', press send. We discovered the sound we wanted, unpolished and raw, in the middle, broken-down section of our 2016 tour. And we found its aching and raised heartbeat there, too.

The songs were on trucks going by, in playgrounds, in paintings, on walls, in photos, in headlines, and waiting at the school gate. They were in lost innocence and the guilt felt when you watch, blink and turn away. And they were in the cold and rigid hands that gripped my heart in a vice, a year on from Daddy's death. A year, I have found, till you wake with their voice, at last, in your ear again.

Close your eyes to keep it. There you are. I miss you. Say it's gonna be all right.

'Road to Eden'

So many tears
In holy water
So much fear in Heaven's way
I ask you when
When will I grow up to not be afraid
And be who I am
Cherish what you left
Courage is all I'm asking tonight
The candlelight dances
Breath of an angel whispering white
It's gonna be all right
It's gonna be all right
Say it's gonna be all right
It's gonna be all right

There's only a long road to Eden
A mountain to climb
But I'm gonna find my way back home
We're not alone when we're lonely
Alone when we cry
Together we'll find a way back home

So here's where you find me
In a rainy day
Doors are closed
Can't come out to play
Tears on the pages
For all that is given
Is taken away
And what's it all for
What's it all for
When inside out
Begins with joy
And sadness a stranger
Till he overwhelms you
Leaving you raw

And here is where the unloved, unwanted and voiceless, in the back corner of the classroom, with a finger on the lips, found their moment.

A trad piece Caroline had written on the piano two years ago, at last liberated, and loved by each of us, to grow into 'The Son of Solomon'. And what a moment. For the hands that were to so delicately touch it, like it was something sacred, were to be those of T Bone Burnett.

And all the while, I am people-watching because I love people-watching. I sit above on my balcony as they leave the football game. Three white-haired, bowed men. A woman pushing another in a wheelchair adorned in Chelsea blue. Two girls laughing at a text one is reading.

Five boys on phones. Because there are always many more there than who we merely see. Those they are walking towards, those they have left, those they are missing, those who are virtually heard.

And every day, these days, there are moments when I really see that we are all one, and connected and never alone in our blood and beat. Walking down down down under *Blade Runner* London onto the Jubilee line train to St John's Wood, and a tap on my shoulder from a stranger alerting me to the wonder of the white feather he had watched dancing on my hair the whole way down. And then, on the train, Tom Petty's 'It's Good to Be King' in my ears. Alone in a rattling carriage but for a black man who is looking elsewhere, opposite me. And then it gets overwhelmingly loud as the old train screeches through a tunnel, the song reaches that heavenly ending and we look at each other and we see. I cried watching him leave, and he stopped. He turned and he waved at me.

We recorded 'Bulletproof Love' that day.

And then another time ascending into the light of a brave new world to recognise Johnny's back. At that moment I was his angel, the white feather dancing on his hair. For I came upon him disoriented, as if heaven sent.

'Don't play that again,' T Bone said in a rehearsal studio in Shepherd's Bush, London. Beneath the arch of another train line, where we rehearsed the record for two weeks before we went in to RAK Studios for another two, to record *Jupiter Calling*. Together, Robbie Malone taking Keith's place on bass, and the right-hand pillar, Anto, still with us on lead guitar, we recorded as live, reel to reel, like an old Beatles record. Windowed, fairy-lit booths separating us. Anomalies and imperfection revered. Capturing the unrehearsed truth. Ritualistic with the scent of the burning Peruvian wood.

And I like to close my eyes to see now, like Daddy towards his end. Till they'll close at last and see forever. And maybe they see me, a dark-haired girl standing small on a chair, trying to see through the sepia. The gauzed and clouded veil into them. Gerry and Jean with Gerard in between them. But I find I can't help living, as they couldn't help dying, and the living don't belong with the dead.

I bring Jeanie and Brett to Sunday Mass, too, like Daddy did us. I am not quite as gothic nor as troubled. And my head is held high because I can't blame God for human fallibility, and if I lost Him, would that not be the greatest casualty? I am afraid it would be for me. Because the truth is, I feel something in churches. A sense of being lovingly watched and an away far beyond where they are, which I just might reach if I listen and believe enough. The heartfelt prayers hang in the frankincense still. I breathe them. They are still in the puff of the once-flamed candle. I breathe out the tears. Breathe out the begging, the forgiveness, the acceptance, the gratitude, the end ... The beginning ... And they form as ghostly

217

spectres once more, only to dissolve as they rise up and disappear.

I feel it. I feel them. I am them.

'And in her sleep that night, in her lost old home, her own mama smiled radiantly upon the hope and blessed it ...'

Dreaming me ...

And the children? Well ... Booboy this morning lit a candle and I watched his little mouth as it said:

'Holy God, I pray that Michael Jackson is alive.'

The hiccups must have got him in the end ...

Right now they are playing football in the living room and talking about some guy called Mr Fartbottom. And they are naked. I won't see this forever. Naked babies I dreamed of.

And what of our own house of God now? Where we were babies and toddlers and children and teenagers and ... a band? Caroline was born in their bedroom upstairs while Daddy played the organ below. But our once-home feels like it remains ever in the respectful and solemn gloaming. Even when I turn the lights on and Daddy's RTÉ Radio 1 (ah, that's what he was trying to do, too) ... As though the life that buzzed in its rooms had all the time been what had lit them up. Had always been its music. It would take a new family to light it up again. Not necessarily to the soundtrack of a family band.

As I write, I know Jaws the organ yawns open in the back of the living room, ever awaiting the touch of young fingers on its cha-cha-cha button. Gaping eager to watch just one more giddy giggle dance. I see the spectre of a grey-socked foot tap-dancing the bass pedals. Left black shoe dismissed for the present, but there it waits … A garda síochána off duty. At ease.

There's no chicken on the tap, nor peeled potatoes in the water, nor the echo of voices in the hall. No tinkling piano, no scales, nor keys demented. No confiscated records between the dresser and the wall. There's no odd socks in the hot press, made even under the beds. There's no lost scissors, no everything drawer, no Blu-Tack on the walls, no school bags dumped in the hall, no burning toast, no bumping chair. There's no open-closing doors, no footprints on the floors, no clothes on the radiators … All is sad and silent beneath a grieving ephemeral dust sheet.

Imagine, though, it happened. A new family moved in (I feel baa sad for the poor house if it doesn't) and the walls recognised a song someone played. 'Time to Say Goodbye'. And they contracted as if to hug themselves in memory of Jean, who danced to that song on repeat one night, about a year before she … said goodbye. And of the family that had grown together between and before them. In dignified mourning the house put a light out forever the day we came home without her. Its first surrender.

No … Not its first …

I had a vivid dream of her about a year after she died. We were seated, all of us, around the kitchen table …

rectangular oak then, and our school uniforms were drying on the radiator behind Caroline and Sharon. I was at one end, facing Daddy, and Mammy was to my right in her seat. I was crying because I knew in the dream that she had died and that she was really gone from us. She hushed me so gently and said, 'Don't cry, Andrea. There's no need to cry any more.'

Don't let it drop. We all held this cup together, from the son of Solomon, chasing shadows down the road to Eden and a love divine, to finish ...

free-falling with ...

the sun and the moon.

For pop can be like a too-tight dress.

You can't really breathe.

Or maybe you outgrow it ...

I woke this morning,
   the day we leave,
sat up in my bed,
with the memory of a last breakfast
and hands, his bitten nails,
on an orange being peeled for me.
Oh Daddy
You are the previous pilgrim

'Water into Wine'

He travels without moving
Under raven skies
And a voice like a viola
I love to madness
You don't meet him
But he happens
Like a storm in the night
On a full-moon Tuesday
In September

I feel feel you
In the corner of my room
You turn water into wine
I feel feel you
Tonight

Dust sheet on the piano
And the curtains drawn
And the emptiness present
Like a rain cloud
Am I baptised or do I drown
It's a curious line
But I miss you to madness
To imagined ...

Swan-song d'Amour

Has the little bird found her voice in a swan-song? The echo of a lead scrawl on the flutter-wings of paper. Born to sing. To fly cry die in a London kitchen cupboard.

'Please Release Me, Let Me Go …'

A lament today, as the sacred wasn't heard because it too was locked dark, too close and elbowing in a cupboard. Or did it ever make it there at all? To the 'Ah, well, tell me mister, where do we put the write-offs?' closet?

Isn't that a striking colour of red on your one in the middle?

Which one is that?

Don't ask me sure I can only tell who Jim is.

There's a brother?!

Haha, you! SLTH.

Was it even real? Was it a pretend record like I thought our very first was when I held it in these same hands, then palm-lined twenty-one years. Fingers leafed through to find it and look, ah, it has its own proper place with its own legitimate file name.

The Corrs.

Corrus, Corr by 4, 4 by Corr (ideal for those cross-country journeys), Corrnucopia (come on now, close that encyclopaedia), Corrupt, Rotten to the Corr (haha,

223

Johnny, will ye stop, for 4 Corrs' sake) … How do ye like them apple … corrs …

We need a name that says who we are …

I suppose that's it so.

That was easy, smiles Gerry Corr, born of the late James and Alice, and a celestial 'Alleluia' descends from the church of the latter-day Corrs in an unholy boast, and a big resounding pro for the family band pros and cons question reveals itself.

Or is it a dream? Will I wake up in a bed in Georgetown, Washington DC, with a prince for a president? Baby-pink marshmallow breath cooing 'Oidle oidle' in a hand-me-down bassinet beside me, and act two has yet to play?

It's January now and it's over.

I'll hold the vinyl of *Jupiter Calling* in my hands (palm-lined forty-three) when I get home, I've decided.

Is this a lament?

No.

This is our triumph.

Radadadada swan-song swan-song d'amour

'Fair play to yiz now … I always thought yizzerzer music was crap, no harm to yiz, but yizzers have done well for yourselves so yiz have.'

And her discovered wonder whispers on, in a car pulling a trailer towards home.

If this is a song
  It's a love song
  It's a song of praise
  For Jean Bell and Gerry Corr
  My brothers Jim and Gerard
  My sisters Sharon and Caroline
  John 'Johnny' Hughes
  And of course
  You …

More hooks than a Russian fishing trawler!!

Acknowledgements

My love and thanks to all those who made this book possible.

Thanks to my manager John Hughes and my publisher Eoin McHugh who believed from the start.

My thanks and appreciation to everyone at HarperCollins. In London: Sarah Hammond, Amber Burlinson, Claire Ward, Vicky Eribo, Carly Cook, Fionnuala Barrett, Alan Cracknell, Dean Russell, Dawn Burnett and Lucy Brown. In Dublin: Tony Purdue, Patricia McVeigh, Nora Mahony, Jacq Murphy and Ciara Swift.

Thanks to Brian Brady and Emmet J. Driver at Dubray.

And thanks to Ann Harrison, Liam Collins and Anna Lucy Hughes.

List of Portraits